EXPLAINING DIVORCE TO CHILDREN

EXPLAINING DIVORCE TO CHILDREN

EDITED BY EARL A. GROLLMAN

WITH AN INTRODUCTION
BY *Louise Bates Ames*

BEACON PRESS, *Boston*

To the Beth El Family
of Belmont, Massachusetts
for eighteen years of understanding and challenge

CONTENTS

Foreword   ix

Introduction by Louise Bates Ames   xi

Prologue   3

   I. CHILDREN IN DIVORCE: AN OVERVIEW
     by *Jetse Sprey*   42

  II. EXPLAINING DIVORCE TO YOUNG CHILDREN
     by *Evelyn Goodenough Pitcher*   63

 III. THE EFFECT OF DIVORCE UPON THE PERSON-
     ALITY DEVELOPMENT OF CHILDREN AND
     YOUTH by *Graham B. Blaine, Jr.*   76

  IV. DIVORCE AND THE CHILD: "THE FATHER QUES-
     TION HOUR" by *Stanley H. Cath*   86

   V. THE CHILD AND LEGAL PROCEDURES OF DI-
     VORCE by *Haskell C. Freedman*   122

  VI. PARENTS WITHOUT PARTNERS—WITH CHIL-
     DREN OF DIVORCE by *Ralph Ober*   142

 VII. A MINISTER'S VIEWS ON CHILDREN OF DIVORCE
     by *Wayne E. Oates*   157

VIII. A PRIEST'S VIEWS ON CHILDREN OF DIVORCE
     by *John L. Thomas*   179

  IX. A RABBI'S VIEWS ON CHILDREN OF DIVORCE
     by *Earl A. Grollman*   201

x. CHILDREN OF DIVORCE, THEIR PERSONAL
   VIEWS: "WOULD A BROKEN HOME BREAK
   YOU?"   232

Notes, References, Bibliographies   246

FOREWORD

MARRIAGE HAS BEEN described as the one enterprise in which we expect 93% of our people to enter and 100% to be successful.

When a marriage begins to founder, couples with children face three difficult choices. They may decide to "stick it out" for the sake of the children; they may try the long and painful process of repairing the marriage; or one or both parents may decide to obtain a divorce.

Divorce may solve many problems. But, inevitably, it creates a new set of dilemmas, particularly where children are involved. There are the practical questions of custody, support, and remarriage. There are the emotional problems of guilt, bitterness, and hostility. The world of the single parent is society's never-never land. It is fraught with social isolation, frustration, and loneliness.

How, then, to face with our children the stormy turbulence of life in a changing and insecure world? It is to suggest approaches to this complex problem that specialists from many disciplines of life are sharing their most knowledgeable views and recent research.

EARL A. GROLLMAN

INTRODUCTION

WHETHER IT IS BETTER for an incompatible couple with children to stay together or to separate depends largely on what is wrong with the marriage. But in general it is now assumed that children are probably better off if totally incompatible parents separate rather than remain together. Even if this is so, divorce is seldom easy for children. Divorcing parents need all the help they can get in smoothing the way for their children. *Explaining Divorce to Children* provides such help.

Nothing is more disturbing to a child than a change he does not understand. Thus one of the most important cautions to any divorcing parent is to be sure that she or he (both if possible) make perfectly clear to the children involved just why the divorce is taking place and, even more important, just exactly what it will mean to them in terms of actual, practical living.

The authors give much good and specific advice and many practical rules for telling children about divorce and for helping them to accept it. The contributors make it quite clear that in the long run it is not so much what parents say as what they are that counts, not so much what parents do at a given time as how they have related with their children that determines how well the reality will be accepted. The authors emphasize that parents should live with their children during the good times in such a way that if bad times come, the relationship will stand up under the strain; and they stress the fact that some children can and will accept a difficult family situation better than others.

As Editor Grollman points out, it is the hope of the authors that in reading this book parents will find, if not answers, stimulation to think through and solve some of the many problems which divorce provokes. This holds true not only for those parents actually divorcing but for others as well. If society accepted divorce more fully and appreciated more generously the problems which it raises, the burdens of the divorced parent and the children involved would be much less heavy.

This is a book which will not only inform and advise the divorcing parent but will also hearten her or him. It not only assures readers that divorce need not be ultimately damaging but reports research showing that, contrary to popular opinion, there is significantly less juvenile delinquency among children of one-parent homes than among those living with both their parents.

That is, it helps debunk the old-fashioned notion that even highly incompatible parents must stay together for the sake of the children. As the authors point out, our society has not yet entirely succeeded in institutionalizing divorce, but this book is a strong first step.

More than anything else so far available, *Explaining Divorce to Children* faces this whole difficult problem in a realistic, positive, and encouraging way. It assures divorcing parents that all is not lost. It helps them by giving specific suggestions as to what to say and to do. And, especially, it helps them appreciate that if they are sound, secure individuals and have done a reasonably good job in raising their children, there is a better than average chance that both they and their children will successfully survive the ordeal of divorce.

LOUISE BATES AMES

EXPLAINING DIVORCE TO CHILDREN

PROLOGUE

"MY SON IS LOST TO ME FOREVER. He is not dead. He is just gone. Nobody except a divorced person can know fully what that means," lamented a divorced father over the severed relationship with his child.

The significance of divorce lies mainly in what it does to all who are involved. It is a major emotional upheaval, a time of radical change, requiring the most difficult and profound adjustments. To husband and wife, it means an end to many cherished hopes and dreams. To children, it may seem like the end of the world.

Youngsters suffer the most serious consequences of divorce. Struggles over their custody, visitation rights, the psychological gap left by one or both missing parents, the agony of having their lives dislocated—all take their toll in future years. Even with the utmost restraint, someone gets hurt: the man, the woman, the parents of the couple, and especially the children. No one can emerge from a divorce unscathed.

The purpose of this book is neither to denounce nor to sanction divorce. Rather it is to speak to those men and women who no longer understand each other and whose love may be gradually turning into hatred. Even though their marriage is failing, there remains crucial unfinished business. First and foremost is the question of whether their

marriage can be saved. But if attempts prove futile and divorce is the unavoidable solution, in what manner should
they tell their progeny about the break-up? How should ex-
husband and ex-wife resolve any differences they may have
about the youngsters—schooling, visitation, and other matters? How does one handle the unavoidable problems of
guilt, bitterness, and hostility?

It is the hope that in reading these chapters, parents will
find, if not answers, stimulation to think through and solve
the weighty problems of family disintegration as it relates to
them and their offspring.

THE PROBLEM

Up to the beginning of this century, divorce presented no
great problem in the United States. There were only 55,751
cases in 1900, or four divorces per 1,000 married couples.
But in 1946, a year of unprecedented marrying and divorcing (both war-generated), divorces totaled 610,000—about
eighteen divorces per 1,000. In 1950, there were 385,000
divorces, or ten per 1,000 married couples.

The United States has the highest divorce rate among
Western nations. Statistics alone do not tell the entire story.
More children have been affected than is sometimes realized. Belying the myth that progeny preserves marriage,
some 60 per cent (versus 42 per cent in 1948) of today's
divorced women have children under 18 at the time of their
breakup. In the Northeast, almost 70 per cent of divorcing
parents have minor children. Today, more than six million
children, nearly one in ten, are living in one-parent homes.

Of new marriages contracted nowadays, it has been estimated that about one-fourth will end in the divorce courts.
In 1964, the latest year for which the Department of Com-
merce has complete figures, there were 1,720,000 mar-

riages and 428,000 divorces, roughly a 4-to-1 ratio. These figures do not take into account the number of permanent separations or of desertions—often called the poor man's divorce—which are believed to equal the number of legal divorces.

CAUSES

Marriage and family living must be understood in relation to the times. They are determined by cultural attitudes as well as by world events. They reflect the conflict between former established family patterns geared to an earlier economy and the needs of today's rapidly changing social scene. The transition from an established to a yet untried value system constitutes one of the most important challenges that marriage faces today.

In this century, revolutionary discoveries and global interaction have had a terrific impact on our lives. One expert observes: "In a few short years, the solidarity of the world has vaporized into a nightmare of uncertainty." The social aspects of the business cycle, which used to concern us so much, seem almost trivial when compared to world conflicts, the draft, and prodigious advances in science and technology, as well as the changing role of women in American life.

Until the mid-nineteenth century, divorce was almost solely the prerogative of the husband. Infidelity and desertion remained a woman's main grounds for obtaining a divorce. Even then she was largely denied the right to property and to bring suit.

Aware that their only means of sustenance was in marriage, women quietly endured their injustice until industrialization provided economic emancipation. As they left the hearth for the office or factory, they were no longer content to endure cruelty or general unhappiness. Today, they

demand more from marriage than economic security, legal-
ized sex relations, or quiet domesticity. Marriage is more
than an "endurance race." They rightfully expect love, affection, and personal satisfaction. Their conviction is that a
sound marriage must be built on the sharing of common
goals and common interests for *female* as well as male. All
this represents a comparatively new attitude toward marriage. It has resulted in dissatisfaction with those marriages
which would have been regarded as successful a half-
century ago. That is why the divorce rate does not necessarily imply that there are more unhappy marriages. It may
simply mean that more people who are unhappily married
today seek divorce because they find less reason to stay
married. Women demand not only equality within marriage
but the right to dissolve an unhappy marriage because of
"contrariety of mind" (incompatibility). During the process
of rapid social and economic revolutions, legislatures have
tended to favor more liberal divorce laws too, for both
wife and husband.

Courts now grant divorce on many legal grounds. These
include adultery, cruelty, desertion, drunkenness, nonsup-
port, neglect to provide, insanity, conviction of a felony, and
other specific acts which are regarded as a violation of the
marriage contract. Cruelty accounts for about 50 per cent
of all divorces; desertion, for about 33 per cent; neglect,
eight per cent. Adultery now ranks in fourth place and is becoming less commonly used as the alleged reason for the
failure of the marriage. (Haskell C. Freedman cites in detail the basic legal principles and procedures of divorce.)

Obviously, the underlying reasons for divorce are as
diverse as the reasons for unhappy marriages. A psychiatric
study of 100 men and women shows that temperamental differences, sexual dissatisfaction, and lack of personal freedom
are by far the most common sources of conflict in marriage.

Sociological findings demonstrate that no matter what the legal grounds, divorce is usually the result of profound tensions that cause the breakdown of the marriage. Strains are traced to difference in cultural background and modes of living and personal habits, as well as variations in attitudes, values, and ideals. Investigations have shown that people who have similar education, religious affiliation, and family backgrounds have a better chance of making their marriage succeed. Also, husbands and wives who share a great many activities, enjoy the same things, and have the same friends tend to be more happily married than those who do not have these things in common.

Other characteristics associated with a compatible marriage beside similarity of background (homogamy) include the length of acquaintanceship prior to marriage (Burgess-Cottrell study finds a long acquaintance is more favorable); engagement of six months or more prior to the wedding; age at marriage with males on the average of 23 years and females at 20; products of happy homes where the parents are relatively compatible (Dr. William Goode has discovered in his classic study of 425 formerly married women in Detroit that divorce breeds divorce. More than half of his subjects were the offspring of broken marriages; in addition, the percentage of those whose own children eventually chose divorce was noticeably higher than the norm); approval of the marriage by family and friends; and the understanding of husband and wife as to role expectations and obligations.

Urban centers make it difficult for married couples to share much of their lives. As a case in point, marriages of farmers are more stable than those of other groups, the farmers having only one-half their proportionate share of divorces. Reasons attributed include the fact that those in rural areas are more likely to participate in joint ventures and have common interests in home, work, and children.

Familistic concepts are linked to the rural society whereas individualistic values are associated with modern urban life.

Our world is changing rapidly, and marriage is in a process of adjusting to these changes. The family, like other institutions, is in a process of flux. New pressures are causing strain and tension in the relationship between husband and wife. Most people have been drawn to the factories and dwell in congested quarters in the cities. Financial insecurity has added to the problem. Although most couples earn enough to "get by," surveys show that families feel they need 50 to 100 per cent more to be comfortable and believe that they really cannot get along with their present income.

Convention is no longer the powerful factor it once was. New values and new ethical standards have developed. If a marriage is too restrictive and too binding on the individual, the result is often divorce. Many still agree with Dr. Lawrence S. Kubie, clinical professor of psychiatry at the University of Maryland, that "divorce is always a tragedy no matter how civilized the handling of it, always a confession of human failure, even when it is the sorry better of sorry alternatives." But Americans are more relaxed, tolerant, and realistic about divorce than they used to be. Though vestiges of social stigma still remain in small communities, most of the nation long ago decided that a happy divorce is better than an unhappy marriage—or, as British author A. P. Herbert called it, "holy deadlock."

Although a number of factors have been investigated for their bearing on marital happiness, no one social force has been isolated which shows an unequivocal relationship with divorce rates. Any one factor may be countered by elements representing opposed forces. In the words of Spinoza: *Omne determinato est negatio* (Any definition is a limitation). Valid controls are lacking. Cause-and-effect relationships are virtually impossible to isolate. The complexity of our society results in great variation in marital patterns. One must understand the unique problems of *each* individual couple to properly evaluate and diagnose the most beneficial assistance for a given, specific, conflicted marriage.

BEFORE DIVORCE

It is impossible to make any general statement about whether a couple should remain together for the sake of the youngsters. What is better for the children depends on what is wrong with the marriage.

Divorce may solve many problems. But inevitably, it creates a new set of enigmas, particularly where youngsters are involved. There are the practical questions of custody, support, and possibly remarriage, along with the unconscious feelings of guilt, failure, and revenge.

Have the conscientious parents really made every effort to rescue their marriage? Have they developed proper insight and objectivity? Have they attempted a new or different relationship with each other and at the same time avoided or possibly courageously faced their disruptive situations? Have they sought professional help, and sincerely tried to help themselves?

It is important to note that six out of seven divorced persons eventually remarry and then proceed to divorce again at the rate of two out of five. The statistics for third marriages are even more dismal; one study found that eight out of ten remarriages involving the twice-divorced failed. The trend raises the question of whether the old explanation for chronic divorce—"You can shed your mate, but not your neurosis"—still applies.

In a marriage which has little or no foundation for future happiness, careful consideration must be given to all of the other reality factors and values involved in husband and wife being permanently separated. For example, outside the courtroom many a newly divorced woman discovers that things are not what she deemed. "While she's married," says Dr. Charles Mahl, a Los Angeles psychiatrist, "the woman sets up elaborate fantasies about being a divorcee. After divorce, her illusions are shattered. She failed to consider the paradox that the law favors the woman but society favors the man."

Many a man also becomes quickly disillusioned. While he might have welcomed the retreat to a free and independent "adolescence," he may find that after a brief and perhaps exciting respite, he is now alone and lonely. He misses the cries of his infant and even the arguments with his ex-wife. He lacks roots and feels that he is cast adrift without a rudder or direction. What he formerly thought he despised he may now crave and desire, but it is too late.

The most immediate cost to both man and woman is the loss of old friends. One clergyman estimates that 90 per cent of a divorcing couple's friends either ostracize both or rally round the husband. Especially the divorcee, explained University of Chicago sociologist Professor Fred L. Strodtback, is often anathema to married couples. She embodies the tensions that they may be feeling but are trying to overlook. Wives, suspicious of the divorcee's motives, misinterpret her most casual gestures toward their husbands. Husbands, meanwhile, assume she is in a perpetual state of aroused sexuality.

If there were monetary problems prior to divorce, this issue can become even more intensified. After all, if there was not enough money before, or barely enough, how can one support two families on the same salary? What will happen to the woman who wed when young and never held a job? Who will take care of the children while she is working? Is divorce then the best solution for the couple?

Divorce does not just "happen." There are obvious distress signals which reveal marital difficulties in their early beginnings. This is the time for the husband and wife to attempt to resolve their difficulties. One need not wait for a cold to become pneumonia before he sees his physician. When serious misunderstandings first arise, this is the time to attempt to save the marriage. If the husband and wife are unable to resolve their dilemmas, there is the possibility of help through individual or group psychotherapy, family service agencies, and religious guidance.

But few in domestic discord avail themselves of the family agencies or of pastoral or marriage counseling services. Some refuse out of complete ignorance or a misconstrued understanding of the function and purpose of these organizations. Frequently, it is the husband who refuses to seek help, perhaps because our Western culture calls for the man to appear strong and indestructible. Thus, he will not place himself in a position of vulnerability.

Many a thwarted woman will ask: "Then why should I go alone to seek help?" Her frustration is understandable. The marital problem is that of husband and wife. But what does she gain by not receiving objective advice from an insightful counselor? A reasoned decision must be made not only for herself but for her offspring as well.

Often a reluctant husband will accept counseling after his wife has made the initial overtures because he now knows that his wife means business and the marriage may in truth be on the verge of collapse. The husband may be apprehensive that he will be the "fall-guy" and held responsible for the family disintegration. The wise therapist can suggest some of the techniques to encourage the absent mate to participate in both diagnosis and therapy.

Professional counseling has certain definite attributes. It is a learned art in which a professionally trained person has acquired basic knowledge, skills, and attitudes. He has integrated them into a disciplined capacity with an understanding of the reciprocal nature of interaction patterns in marriage. His goal is to help both partners come to some awareness of the appropriateness or inappropriateness of their own feelings, demands, and expectations. He assists them in resolving or handling more adequately those factors which cause the domestic discord.

There are many kinds of marriage counseling. *Classical psychoanalysis* provides an intensive individually oriented approach. *Collaborative* therapy ("stereoscopic technique") includes the utilization of the team approach, with marital partners treated by different psychiatrists who are in constant communication for the purpose of maintaining the marriage. In *concurrent* counseling both partners are treated by the same therapist, but at a different time; the therapist is thus able to achieve a multidimensional view of the entire marital disharmony. Both husband and wife are seen together by the same counselor in *conjoint* marital therapy. Moreover, many therapists have integrated a *combined approach* which allows greater flexibility in dealing with the personality and situation of the counselees.

It is impossible to suggest which approach is best. Not only are there differences in method and technique of treatment but also profound variations among therapists of the so-called same theoretical system in terms of knowledge, skill, pliability, and personal aptitudes. Often the family physician is one who is aware of the specific needs of the couple and can help make a proper referral. Some major cities maintain a competently staffed professional organization, i.e., a Family Service Society, to aid people in marital trouble. Other agencies that may be able to help include the Child Welfare League, the National Association for Mental

Health, the American Medical Association, as well as the local health and welfare departments.

One of the most promising developments in the handling of divorces is the family court with professional counselors as part of a "conciliation service." Interestingly enough, this progressive approach is being largely pioneered in the South, West, and North. Little has been attempted along these lines in the East.

The most notable of the court counseling services is that of Judge Paul W. Alexander in Toledo, Ohio. His unusual counseling facility is housed in an impressive $1,500,000 building known as the Family Court Center. Customary legal facilities have been provided along with working space for a psychiatrist, marriage counselors, psychologists, a pediatrician, a nurse, and other operating personnel.

The profession of marriage counselor is a comparatively new one but has proven to be extremely helpful, especially for short-range supportive therapy. Unfortunately, exacting standards of training, education, and experience have not always been established for persons assuming this role.

Clergymen have traditionally assisted those in marital conflict. Clinical training for a limited number of Protestant seminary students was launched in 1925 and became absorbed into the curriculum of the Episcopal Theological Seminary of Cambridge, Massachusetts. It was the eminent Dr. Richard Cabot who proposed a Clinical Year for Theological Students at an Atlantic Coast Inter-Seminary Conference in New York City. His argument was that the clergyman who graduated from a theological seminary should no more step out into full responsibility as pastor of a church than a medical school graduate should go directly into the private practice of medicine without having had at least a year to learn under supervision.

Despite the fact that the minister is not a medical therapist, he may be of unique assistance. He represents a concerned religious community. His truest function is revealed
in terms of years and decades, as he watches children grow,
marries them, and teaches their children in turn. He is minister, pastor, counselor to individuals and families in joy
and adversity. He attempts to support his people by giving
them a spiritual insight into their inner conflicts.

Since divorce encompasses more than the spiritual and
psychological, the couple should also speak to an attorney
or separate attorneys before contemplating divorce. Laws
regarding divorce and custody differ from state to state.
Please note: it is unconscionable for parents to involve their
children in the legal procedure of divorce!

If divorce is imminent, make sure that the lawyer is both
experienced and trustworthy. You must be completely candid about all your personal and financial matters, even the
most intimate "closet skeletons." Many a case has been lost
because the client had tried to withhold vital information
only to discover that the opposing attorney was not only
aware of the "secret" facts but utilized this very material to
win his case.

Before divorce, consult those competent experts who may
be of assistance in evaluation and guidance. Be aware of all
the ramifications that will touch your own future as well as
that of your offspring. Much is at stake. This may be the
most important decision of your life.

Should the couple remain together for
the sake of the children?

Of course, children growing up in homes that have experienced divorce may have a greater struggle to achieve
satisfactory adjustments than youngsters who grow up in
homes where both mother and father are present. But like all

generalizations, there are many exceptions. The young persons may well be more damaged by living in an armed camp where parents are in constant warfare. The presence of two "partners" in the home is no guarantee either of happiness for the adults or of a wholesome climate in which the children can mature and develop to their full potential.

A marriage that is doggedly maintained "for the sake of the children" could create more severe problems, not only for the parents but, through them, for the children. Youngsters with one loving parent may be better off than those with two who use their offspring as pawns in their struggle for mastery over each other. Thus, a broken home is not the only cause of youngsters' troubles. They may feel terribly guilty that the family remains intact only because of them. It has been said that children may thrive better as orphans of divorce than as members of a family always mobilized for combat.

Dr. J. Louise Despert, child psychiatrist, was one of the first to point out that the "emotional divorce" of parents could be far more devastating to children than actual divorce. "Astonishingly," she wrote, "I found far fewer children of divorce among these disturbed youngsters than are found proportionately among the general population, which includes both well-adjusted children and children in difficulties. There was trouble between the parents of every one of the children in my files, but surprisingly few of them had been divorced."

Later research supported these findings. A study published by Professor Ivan Nye of the State College of Washington indicates that children of divorced parents suffer less from psychosomatic ailments, are less inclined toward delinquency, and have a better relationship with their parents than children whose parents quarrel perpetually. Dr. Nye concludes that our thinking concerning broken homes is in need of revision. "Failure to perceive the good adjustment both of children and spouses in many broken homes may stem from a concentration upon the tensions which occur at the time of the break. After a period of adjustment, a new equilibrium is established, complicated perhaps by the necessity for each family member to play new and less clearly defined roles, but largely free of the unbearable conflicts of the previous unhappy marriage."

Dr. William A. Goode of Columbia University agrees. He writes: "Unfortunately for those who seek easy solutions of family disorganization, it also seems likely that a family in which there is continued marital conflict, or separation, is more likely to produce children with problems of personal adjustment than a family in which there is divorce or death. . . . The choice usually has to be between a continuing conflict or a divorce. And the evidence so far suggests that it is the conflict of divorce, not the divorce itself, that has an impact on the children."

In a recent work by Iowa State University sociologist Lee Burchinal, two large groups of seventh- and eleventh-grade students whose parents had been divorced were compared with classmates from the whole spectrum of intact homes, happy and unhappy. Dr. Burchinal detected no significant difference in the emotional health of the two groups.

These experts are stating that a divorce can be a difficult blow for the children, but they are also suggesting that it can be *more* security-shaking if they remained in a home with nameless tensions, smoldering resentments, and incompatibilities too deep to be reconciled.

Nor must the separation inevitably warp the youngsters' development. Children of divorce do have emotional problems, but so do youngsters of happy homes. Not long ago it was usually assumed that the child of divorce was destined for the police station. Clearly some end up there. In their book *Unraveling Juvenile Delinquency,* Sheldon and Eleanor Glueck reported finding 21 per cent of delinquent children from homes where the parents were separated or divorced. However, in almost every case other factors also figured prominently, in particular either the economic situation or the physical condition of these broken homes. Almost every scientific investigation has concluded that most youngsters of divorce turn out emotionally sounder than those living in the twilight of a discordant marriage.

Is it better for parents who are unhappily married to stick it out together for the sake of the children? In trying to answer this question, ask yourself: "What are the emotional needs of my youngsters at their particular ages? Are they truly being met in our home?" "Are we remaining together for some well-intentioned martyrdom?" "Is there some degree of warmth, love, and sharing or is it just an 'empty shell' of separate individuals exposing the youngsters to a shared contagion of pain, humiliation, despair?"

Some whose marriages are hopelessly beyond repair do not seek out the divorce courts because they say they must remain together "for the sake of the children." Is this true? Or is it their excuse and rationalization? Are they really staying together because they fear the uncertainty of the unknown? They may dread the reactions of family and friends. They may panic because of economic considerations. They may be terror-stricken at the thought of aloneness. Admittedly, these are all sizable factors that must be thought through before a lasting decision of divorce. But why make the children the scapegoat? If truth be known, breaking up, rather than continuing a seriously unhappy marriage "for the sake of the children" may frequently be the more merciful course.

(Graham Blaine and Evelyn Pitcher believe that, if at all possible, a divorce should be delayed until the child reaches a certain age.)

WHEN THE DECISION IS DIVORCE

Before discussing the breakup with your offspring, make sure that the decision is irrevocable. There is nothing more devastating for a child than to be informed about a divorce that is only being discussed as a possibility. It is a cruel mistake to announce a breakup which was discussed the previous night during a ferocious quarrel. Take heed that you never in anger or haste bandy the word "divorce." If the parents do reconsider and decide to maintain the marriage, the youngsters could well develop a pathological dread that even an ordinary argument could lead to separation. After hearing the term "divorce" in the household, a boy of eight had difficulty at mealtime. If the father jokingly criticized the wife's cooking, the remark was conjured up as a threat to the future stability of the family. Why inject the possibility of a breakup of the home until it is finally and unalterably agreed upon by both the mother and father?

However, if divorce is imminent, experts have agreed that it is best to tell the children at once. Nothing is more disturbing to young people than to feel shut out and ignored. A woman once confided: "The most miserable experience of my childhood was hearing from my next door neighbor that my parents were going to separate. I felt bad enough for what was happening, but the final humiliation was to have to receive this intimate news from a rank outsider."

In breaking the news to the children, remember that truth is always the best formula. Evasions and half-truths only return to haunt those involved—both parents and children. To make the story creditable, more and more fabrications have to be added to the original deceit. The mother who tells the youngster, "Daddy is away on a business trip," must someday face up to the "time that he will return." Understandably, the child develops the delusion that someday the father will come back to the house and family life will again be normal.

Never cite an untruth that the child must unlearn for himself. Initially, it may be easier for the parent to respond to the agony of breakup with fiction. But if you expect your child to be honest with you, you must be honest with him. Ultimately your falsehoods will bring confusion, misconception, and mistrust.

It is futile to think that the parents' emotional upheaval can remain secret. Even the child who is too young to ask in words and too immature to understand a complicated explanation, may feel the many curious and even frightening changes taking place. He perceives what is going on around him—how often do parents observe the youngster giggle simply because the adults around him are laughing. The child is aware of sadness as well as happiness. He detects inflections not only by the tone of the parents' voices but even in the manner in which he is lifted from his crib. The mother may hold him stiffly, without the usual warmth of maternal relationship. He detects the absence of the father. When there is tension, the youngster reacts to the cheerlessness of the environment. His own emotional disturbances might be indicated by fidgeting and restlessness, withdrawal, regressive thumb sucking, excessive crying, or by destructive behavior directed against toys and other objects. The manner in which divorce is discussed with the youngster may well determine his future mental health.

Telling the children about the divorce
The discussion should not take place after the husband

and wife have been arguing. Too often in this atmosphere
of malevolence, the hysterical parents rush headlong to the
youngsters: "We can't stand it any longer. We're getting
divorced!" Separation and its meaning should be approached
gently and sympathetically during a time of relative relaxation and tranquility.

Difficult as it may be, the explanation should, if possible,
come from both parents. This serves several purposes. It less-
ens the possibility of one partner making the other responsible. By the joint explanation, they together attempt to work
for the best interest and welfare of their offspring. That
means, not letting the progeny become the weapon in the
battle between the parents or asking them to take sides.

The words are, of course, hard to find. They may go
something like this, altered to the vocabulary and understanding of the offspring: "You know we have not been getting along so well. You heard the many times we have been
fighting, haven't you? Now everyone argues from time to
time, like you and your friends. Everyone differs in some
way from everybody else and so it is not wrong to occasionally raise your voice and even be angry. But for us, it is not
just an *occasional* disagreement. It is a *constant* annoyance
and irritation. We are just not happy together. We can't
agree on a lot of important things. We are more often than
not just plain miserable. You could tell, couldn't you, by the
way we are constantly at each other's throat. You saw mom
crying so often. You probably noticed that dad was not
home as often as he used to be, sometimes leaving after a
quarrel.

"In fact, because of our discontent, we are not only miserable to each other but to you as well. We have been cross
with you sometimes for no good reason. Mother and I are
just so unhappy with each other, not with you. You know, if
you don't get a good night's sleep, then you may be grumpy

the next day. That's the way we have been with each other—
growling and irritable and ill-humored.

"I know that you are hearing something that is painful
and difficult for you to understand. But remember that
adults, too, can make mistakes. Your mother and I are
human beings. We have made maybe more than our share of
blunders in our marriage. We're sorry. More than you know.
But the way to correct an error is to change. We don't want
to remain as unhappy as we have been together in the past.
We have thought about it for a long, long time. We have
even seen an expert for help. We have now come to an
important decision—that we would be happier if we (your
father and mother) lived separately.

"But this we want you to know. Even though we may
have taken out our unhappiness on you, we are *not* breaking
up because of you. On the contrary, you're the ones who
have brought joy and meaning to *both* of us. Even though
many things in our marriage were wrong, you were the one
saving feature. You are not to blame for what has happened to our marriage. Let me repeat that again. *You are
not to blame!*

"As far as your mother and I are concerned, there are no
good guys and bad guys. No one who wears a white hat.
Even though we will not be husband and wife, we are still
your parents and will take care of you—that's the one thing
we do agree upon—the children whom we will always love."

The youngsters may respond with tears and pleas. They
may say: "Don't do it. Please! I'll do anything." You should
not counter with lengthy explanations of grievances. This
would only hurt them more. They are really protesting:
"You don't mean it. You said many things before but then
you changed your minds. Won't you reconsider?"

If the decision is firm, then you must not be swayed by
the painful petitions of the youngsters. The children must be

definitely informed on how things stand. Gamesmanship
has ended. It is the time for truth. "We have given it every
consideration. We have thought about it for months. We
tried everything to make it work. We failed. We just can't go
on any longer together." To talk about the possibility of
reconciliation is only to mislead and prolong the agony.

How much in detail do you explain difficulties leading to divorce?

The children have witnessed the conflicts in the home.
They are aware of the many encounters of collision. It is not
necessary nor wise to isolate single issues. You might say:
"You have watched us for so many years, and for so many
reasons you have seen us unhappy." One mother tried to
expound the motive for separation and explained: "We just
can't agree on money. I want to buy clothes and daddy
won't let me." Now, financial considerations may be one of
the difficulties that separate husband and wife; however, by
trying to be specific, the mother oversimplified the problem.
One of the children said: "I know what to do. You, dad,
give her more money and then you won't have to be divorced." The youngest then joined in: "Keep my allowance,
mother. I won't buy any candy. This way you can stay together." In other words, each event when described individually may seem trivial and surmountable. The solitary
skirmish is but a symptom of the overall and complex causes
of the disharmony. Keep the discussion in a general framework.

Always remember to avoid philosophical interpretations.
Words like "incompatibility" and "sociological and psychological factors" give rise to greater confusion than comprehension. Do not tell children what they are unable to
understand. Do not be evasive, but modify explanations

according to the youngsters' discernment. Difficult terms often slip by them as they take only the familiar words to weave them into a meaning of their own.

Questions should be answered in a matter-of-fact way, briefly, without too much emotion. Often the progeny do not ask for details. Because of the parents' own feelings of guilt, they sometimes have the tendency to offer longer and deeper explanations than the children can fathom.

The youngsters may ask that the parents repeat the explanation. Even adults who hear of a crisis may say, "I don't believe it. It can't be true. Say it once more." So, gently, repeat yourself. It is their way of understanding, accepting, coping with, and working through the anxiety situation. Especially the very young do not have great retentive powers. When overwhelmed by mental anguish, they may not absorb everything the first time.

What is said is important, but how it is said has an even greater bearing on whether the children will develop neurotic anxiety or accept within their capacity the fact of separation. The best explanation may be mostly nonverbal. You might hold the youngsters close to you so that they can actually feel your warmth and affection and really know that they are not being forsaken and abandoned.

Why shouldn't the children know the true facts? It was my "ex" who is to blame for the divorce.

Just as the widow or widower is apt to exaggerate the dead spouse's *virtues,* divorced people tend to magnify the other's *faults.* The bereaved feel impelled to deify the deceased. Separated individuals are almost compelled to deprecate the former mate. The widow likes to think that a paragon of virtue married her, for one never dishonors the dead. The divorcee likes to think that she shed a totally mean and rotten person, for what is over must now be good riddance. Either extreme is hard for the children. They are faced with a nonobjective bias of life.

In the grip of their anger, divorced people may lose perspective as far as their offspring are concerned. They try to justify themselves by placing the *entire* blame on the other parent. By disparaging the other mate, they force on their children the painful experiences of having to take sides. The bitter contest between the parents may have a certain harsh logic for them. Divorce does bring feelings of guilt, indignation, and revenge. One method of vendetta is to break down the love of the other and say: "Your father never cared for you." Or, "Your mother is selfish and only thinks about herself." However, the gain is but a temporary release to "get even." It is to "use" children as a vehicle for transmitting contempt and anger. For the children, there is only further insecurity and tension. No youngster likes to think that he was sired by a man who was so completely bad. No child wants to have as support a mother who is insensitive, unfeeling, and self-indulgent. Children may even feel it hopeless to try to be good. They are doomed to be bad like their parents! The offspring need to feel wanted and loved by two parents who are, of course, not angels; but neither are they devils. There is an intolerable hurt when either parent says anything denigrating about the other. It only keeps alive the bitterness and misunderstanding which bring parents and children so much pain in divorce.

On the other hand, you do not have to go overboard in the opposite direction. In covering up your own hostility and hatred for the other partner, you should not present a falsified image of the other's perfection and impeccability. Simply treat your ex-partner with respect and truth.

What is the truth? Both of you are human. No matter what the inadequacies of the absent parent, there are always some positive qualities that might be emphasized. There is no need to blacken each other's character in detail and then ask the children to judge between weaknesses. Just remember, if vindictiveness is manifested, you are not completely emancipated from your former mate. You cannot begin to build a new healthy life until you free yourself from acrimony and revenge.

You keep talking about guilt. I did nothing to be ashamed about. And certainly my children are blameless.

In some ways, the cause of death is easier to explain. A physiological interpretation: "He had cancer." A theological approach: "The Lord giveth, the Lord taketh away." With divorce, physical and religious reasonings are often of little avail.

If the marriage was unsuccessful, one or both parties had to be responsible. Many ex-spouses have fallen asleep thinking, "If only I had treated my husband differently," or "If only I had been more understanding of my wife. Maybe if I had tried a little bit harder, the children wouldn't have to suffer." These thoughts may not be verbalized. Who wants to be culpable and guilty of negligence? Instead these sentiments of personal responsibility are repressed by projecting the complete guilt upon the other partner.

Youngsters often believe that they were the cause of the separation. More than adults, children are apt to feel guilty since in their experience most of the bad things that happen to them, happen because they were naughty. Divorce must be a retribution for their wrongdoings. Therefore, they search for the "bad deed" that caused it. One youngster said: "Don't leave, Daddy, I will put away my toys. I promise, honest."

Young children believe in magic. If one wishes someone harm, the wish will bring results. A little boy once said in anger, "I hope I never see you again." When he learned that the parents were being divorced, the lad felt that his provoking words had brought about the separation. A girl was afraid that her mother knew all about her jealous and possessive feelings concerning her father. After the divorce and the father's leaving home, she actually thought that he had been pushed out of the house to inflict punishment upon her. Guilt may be induced by a misconception of reality.

Resultant behavior varies. There may be aggressiveness with great excitability. There may be unsociability and obvious despondency. There may be a lack of interest in class, or a degree of forgetfulness of ordinary concerns.

Some parents compensate for their guilt by an excessive concern and overprotectiveness and indulge the children by giving them expensive but unnecessary gifts. They feel better by "paying off." However, one cannot purchase affection. The ingredients children need are enduring love and understanding.

What are some other emotional reactions to divorce?

A child's response is a complicated mechanism. He feels distressed that one parent has left the household. The familiar design of family life is disrupted. He also feels sorry for himself because he may believe that he was picked out for personal pain. He is faced with many problems that hopelessly confuse him.

How the youngster reacts depends on many factors: age, custody arrangements, coping mechanisms, relationship between the child and his mother and father. Each experiences the conflict in a different way. Each views it in his own particularity and detail. Each response is unique. Below are some of the well-marked symptoms that divorce *could* cause:

Denial and Silence: Sociologist Judson T. Landis made a

study of 295 undergraduates at the University of California at Berkeley. Findings revealed that after their parents divorced, many students lied about their family and talked as though their mother and father were still living together.

Younger children especially employ the mechanism of denial to protect their ego from disagreeable circumstances. They may react to the disruption of divorce: "I don't believe it. My parents are just having another argument. They won't leave me." The ability to deny unpleasant parts of reality is the counterpart of an hallucinatory wish fulfillment. In a sense, it amounts to closing one's eyes to the real state of affairs.

The child may appear as if he were unaffected by the announcement. The parents have told the offspring about the divorce. With trepidation, they await a thunderous response. The youngster may just say quietly: "O.K. Can I go out and play now?" This does not mean that he is indifferent. He may simply be trying to defend himself against great inner tension by pretending that nothing has really happened. The adult may feel that the youngster's apparent unconcern is insensitive and heartless. Or there may be a wonderful sense of relief. "Isn't it great! He doesn't seem to be the least bit concerned." Not at all. The child's seeming indifference may signify that he has found the disruption too great to accept. He goes on pretending that the breakup did not occur. The pain of anxiety and threat are warded off. It is all dismissed from consciousness. This is why it is so important to help the child accept reality by not further adding to his fantasy world with half-truths and fiction.

If the child is taciturn, do not be discouraged. In the midst of strong emotion, a youngster may have difficulty communicating his feelings. Or he may not want to do so. Be available to him when he might wish to speak his mind— his fears, his guilt, and even his hate. You may penetrate

the language barrier and generation gap by telling him that
you think you know how he must feel because you are upset
too. With your own frank admission, he may finally "open
up." In fact, you may help each other.

Regression: Following the traumatic experience of divorce, children may retreat to earlier stages of development.
They may return to infantile tendencies belonging to the
period preceding the conflict. Regression ensues because of
the failure to master the new anxiety. In light of the hazards
involved, the child is afraid to take the next step. He is more
secure when he retraces back to the time of safety before
the breakup. In the primitive return to earlier forms of
gratification, speech often becomes babyish. Or the child
may suck his thumb, wet his bed, or whine a great deal and
demand the attention of adults.

It must be noted that the various stages of *all* children's
development show a great deal of overlapping and interaction with one another. No phase is ever given up. Sigmund
Freud used the simile of an army. With advancement into
new territory, the soldiers leave strong garrisons en route
serving both to forward supplies and to offer a place of retreat in the event of insuperable difficulties ahead. Even
mature adults sometimes evince immature actions. With
your progeny, there is no need to panic if regressive behavior begins immediately before or after divorce. It may be
the child's way of saying: "Don't leave me. See I am only a
little child. Please love me and stay with me."

Bodily Distress: Children are frightened in a strange unfamiliar world. This feeling is compounded when they suddenly face an unknown universe caused by divorce. Anxiety
could be accompanied by bodily change: trembling, restlessness, loss of appetite, an increase in the rate of the pulse and
respiration, nausea, diarrhea, urinary frequency, and sleep
which is fitful and interrupted by frightening dreams. (Some-

times these dreams become so threatening that the youngster is afraid to fall asleep lest the nightmares begin again.)

Somatic reaction occurs because the child believes himself in danger. No longer is he sure that the needs of food,
shelter, comfort, and love will be forthcoming. He might be
uncomfortable, miserable, and perhaps die. And he has reason to be afraid. It is the burnt child who fears the fire. Since
youngsters are less verbal, their acute anxiety attacks are
often expressed in physical and behavioral symptoms.

Hostility: With divorce, the offspring is threatened with
dislocation and the loss of love. An aggressive desire for
revenge may arise. Angry feelings and angry acts are used
by all of us to remove frustration. When we are enraged,
our first impulse is to strike the person or persons who have
caused us so much suffering. We may not like hostility in
ourselves but we just cannot tolerate it in our children. After
all, they should have positive, loving sentiments for their
family. We do not understand that normal and natural human reality must take account of negative feelings as well.
Our children, like us, have ambivalent feelings, and love
and hate may co-exist in them, too. Where there is devotion, there may be hostility.

The child may interpret the breakup of the home as a
kind of abandonment. He may feel that he has been deserted and betrayed by the ones he loved best and needed
most. He may wish to retaliate against those that would
interfere with his most pressing needs and greatest satisfactions, to get even with them and destroy them! "How could
my father desert me?" "How dare my mother work and
leave me?" He may become so enraged that he may even
attempt to demolish everything around him and eventually
himself.

Some parents unwisely react to this anger by a threat of
further punishment. But the offspring has had enough abuse

and intimidation. Let him know that you understand his feeling of resentment toward you for failing to prevent the breakup. Listen to him if he wishes to tell you about his pain, fears, and animosity. Encourage him to ask further questions and answer them frankly and sympathetically.

Crying: An *affect* is an emotion or feeling tone. Affects include happiness and sadness, elation and depression. We may laugh when we are joyful. We also need to endure the affect of melancholy.

Crying is a natural method of expression. The child feels anxious and guilty—anxious because his future is threatened, guilty because of his actual or imagined role in the domestic strife. And he is afraid. He may cry as he expresses painful emotion. When he gives vent to tears, he feels somewhat relieved. Grief is a different emotion for the child than for the adult. He feels it, but does not know how to verbalize it.

Too often, well-meaning people say: "Be brave! Don't cry! Everything will be all right. Be a man." But everything is not all right. Nor is a youngster an adult. Crying is his sound of anguish at losing a part of the familiar and secure existence. Grief is the human expression of the need for love.

The worst thing possible is for the child to repress his feelings. The youngster who stoically keeps his grief bottled up inside may later find release in a more serious explosion to his inner makeup.

Be realistic enough to say, "Yes, it's difficult. I know you are crying because you care so much. You are not indifferent to what is going on. You feel so strongly because you love us and are afraid." Then make the youngster feel free to express himself. Otherwise the adult deprives him of the relief of giving vent to the affect of sadness.

Panic and Confusion: With divorce, children become uncertain and alone at a time when they most need to feel close to both mother and father. The usual patterns of family life are modified. The youngsters feel anxious: "Who will take care of us now? Where and how will we live?"

After divorce, the children may be exposed to two different sets of values—each of which belongs to a parent. They visit the father and listen to his philosophy of life. They return to their home and observe a totally different mode of behavior. The mother may say: "Be careful that you are not like your daddy." In their confusion, they may swing to and fro, fluctuating indecisively between contradictory feelings and patterns of life.

Older children may become flustered when they envisage their future. They reflect: "When I think of my mother and father's life together, no thanks! Marriage is not for me." A mother may tell her daughter about the utter viciousness of the father. The girl grows up thinking that *all* men are scoundrels. If it is the mother who leaves, the youth may believe that *all* women have a tendency to hurt men. To avoid being wounded by them, he loves them and leaves them. He must act before he is hurt, leave rather than be left.

Parents must therefore be on their guard that they do not malign one another and poison their children's attitude toward all men or women. Children can also be made to understand that because their parents made mistakes, there is no reason to assume that they will make the same ones. A bride once said: "I watched my mother and father and vowed that I would profit from their errors." She made sure that when an argument arose, instead of allowing it to fester for days as did her vindictive parents, she and her husband agreed never to go to sleep without talking it through and making up. She understood that there is a risk to marriage, but so are there hazards in achieving anything worthwhile in life.

The above are some of the responses that children manifest when confronted with divorce. Some reactions come
with the announcement of a divorce. Some, after the separation has taken place. Some may never appear at all. And
some are part of the normal maturation process.

The line of demarcation between "normal psychological
aspects of separation" and "distorted reactions" is thin indeed, just as is the division between "normality" and "neurosis." The difference is not in symptom but in intensity. It is
a *continued* silence and inability to discuss the divorce, or a
prolonged bodily distress, or a *persistent* panic, or an *extended* guilt, or an *unceasing* hostility that is cause for concern. Each manifestation does not in itself determine a
mental illness.

Some danger signals which may indicate that help might
be considered include: delinquency, unwillingness to remain
in school, difficulties in learning, sexual perversion, obses-
sive compulsive reactions, tics or habit spasms, as well as
withdrawal, friendlessness, and uncommunicativeness.

If there are any real doubts, the parent should seek special assistance from the psychologist, psychiatrist, child guidance clinic, or mental health center. This is a time of stress
and strain and your discussions with a sympathetic but objective professional person may bring help not only for your
child but yourself as well.

(Ralph Ober would add a note of caution with what he
describes as the "risk of psychotherapy." Stanley H. Cath,
on the other hand, depicts the inestimable value of counseling for a family of divorce.)

VISITATIONS

Probably the most thorny problem of divorce is the question of visitations. It is usually the mother who has custody

of the children and the father who has the privilege of seeing his youngsters at specific times. The atmosphere is often charged with tension. Formerly married people must now confront each other. They are reminded of bitter moments of strife, contention, and guilt. As they see each other, they realize all too vividly the failures of days gone by. But the past cannot be obliterated. No matter what resentments may exist, the important factor is the best interests of the progeny. Too often, the intractable dispute over visitation privileges stems not from a regard for the children but the unconscious desire of both parents to gain an advantage over the other. When controversies arise over visitation arrangements, the ex-husband and ex-wife each must ask the one overriding question: "What is best for the children?"

Youngsters need a father. He is the male person to imitate, a masculine foil with whom the son can learn to temper feelings of aggression and love. With maternal overprotectiveness, boys sometimes grow into adulthood with emotional ties to the mother which they cannot break or relinquish. Fathers are important also in developing femininity in their daughters. Dr. Loren Mosher of the National Institute of Mental Health found that poverty alone is not as important a factor in juvenile crime as the absence of an understanding and loving father. Even though the father's visitation may be occasional, he can still make his presence felt with the communication of some degree of guidance, security, and protection.

Unfortunately, many men do not accommodate themselves to this vital and irreplaceable role. Some could be categorized as the "Fall-away Father." They don't die. They just "fade away." They keep cropping up from time to time, only to vanish again. They forget important occasions such as birthdays and graduations. They rationalize by saying, "I don't want to interfere with their new life," or "Their mother makes it impossible for me to see them." The real reasons are because the fathers are selfish and irresponsible—and the children become the losers, deprived of a father's attention, knowledge, and direction.

When both former husband and wife are responsible people and realize the offspring's need for a solid and secure relationship with the father, they can amicably work together to make the visitations really meaningful and significant. Visits need careful planning. The father should first clear the time with the mother and children. This would ensure his not upsetting important elements of the youngsters' schedule such as naps, meals, and doctors' appointments.

The father should arrive on time. Don't promise and then be conspicuous by your absence. Your children have had enough disappointments and disillusionment. Youngsters learn to trust by relationships with trustworthy parents.

The mother must be flexible about the children's visitation with the father. Neither youngsters nor the father should be sabotaged by petty rules and unreasonable regulations. Children, however, should be returned before they become weary. A tired youngster can soon forget the amusement and fun he had with dad and recall only his total exhaustion.

Visitations can be a positive and joyous experience for father and offspring. It is not necessary or desirable to spend the time purchasing extravagant gifts, or going to fancy restaurants. You may assuage your guilt but you won't buy love. Remember, even though you are a "Sunday father" you are still a father. Do those things that fathers do best. With a son, give him the image of masculinity. Play ball, attend a football game (and explain it to him as the contest progresses) or assemble a model airplane. The daughter does not need as much physical activity. If she has an interest in dancing, you could go to the ballet. But so often she is just as content to share a quality relationship of conversation and discussion. One girl said: "I like to go to movies. But the time I was happiest was when we window-shopped and talked. I told him about school and my friends. It was groovy."

When the children return to the house, they should not be deluged with questions: "What did you do?" "What did you eat?" "What did he say?" The afternoon's events should be privileged communication. Too often, the youngsters are almost afraid to enjoy themselves for fear that they will once again be part of the "tug-of-war" and that the day will be poisoned by the mother's inquisition, complaints, and criticisms. Nor should the father attempt to obtain "secret" information about the mother's life and actions.

Admittedly, visitation privileges are complicated. But the rewards can be great. In the long run, it is usually best for the children to have the opportunity to reshape their relationship with their nonresident father and realize that they are truly loved and guided by both parents.

(Both Evelyn G. Pitcher and Wayne E. Oates have different views on this subject.)

WHEN THE MOTHER HAS LEFT

Anna Freud points out that a child's first love for his mother becomes the pattern for all later loves. "The ability to love, like all other human faculties, has to be learned and practiced." If this relationship is interrupted by desertion or abandonment, the youngster may do one of four things: remain attached to a fantasy of an idealized mother; invest his love in things (study or work); be frightened to love anyone but himself; or hopefully, accept his loss and find another real person to love.

In a home where there is no mother, there are almost always mother substitutes—a housekeeper, a grandmother, an aunt, an older sister. Thus the children are exposed to inti-

mate personal relationships with some woman, some significant female companionship.

The offspring may become preoccupied with fear for the
health of the father. "Suppose something happens to you,
who will take care of me?" This state of confusion needs the
father's supportive love: "My health is fine. I expect to be
around for a long, long time." Never intimidate the children
with the threat of illness as a result of their mischievous actions. Even so-called idle remarks like, "I get a pain when I
think of all the things I have to do being both mother and
father to you," can bring guilt and panic to the youngsters.

Some "pragmatic" fathers operate on the theory that it is
easier to explain the absence of the mother by using the fiction of death. In this way, the matter is disposed of with
finality. Yet, is it final? "Where is she buried?" "Can I visit
the grave?" Once again, *ad infinitum,* never respond with a
misconception of reality. You only add to the children's own
fantasies, representing a realm halfway between the fully
conscious and the unconscious thought of dreams. Do not
exaggerate their mother's good qualities to a degree completely out of keeping with her real life and character. Neither should you describe her in terms of pure venom. You
may simply say: "Your mother did not leave you to be mean.
She cared about you. But there were so many problems that
she felt it would be best if I took care of you. She knew I
would love and protect you."

BOARDING SCHOOL

Children are subject to two profound fears: the fear of
bodily injury and the fear of the loss of loved persons.

In the case of divorce there is often the feeling that one
has, in truth, lost a loved one. For example, the father may
no longer be living at home and is seen only sporadically. A
youngster may experience guilt, believing that he is respon-

sible for this dislocation and loss. To summarily send him away to boarding school may furnish further proof that he is being punished for his "crime" or that his family just wish to "get rid" of him.

In general, the child should not be exposed to additional readjustments immediately following divorce. He should first be afforded the opportunity to make his own accommodation to the new life in the presence of one parent, and not be "sent away" to a preparatory school where he could well feel total rejection and abandonment. Certainly this is true for the very young, who need the emotional support and security of a loving home and mother.

However, a teen-age boy who has made a relatively good adjustment to the crisis of divorce might still welcome the opportunity of living away, especially if some of his friends are also going to boarding school. But he must understand that he is not being shipped out as a kind of retribution. He should be part of the decision-making process and accompany the parents (preferably) or parent in visitation before selection. The school that is finally chosen should have a homelike atmosphere where he could seek new friends of his own age, and the teachers should be persons who could suitably serve as models for his own future development. Nor should the location be too distant, in order that the youth may occasionally come home for week-ends and vacations. Even though he now lives away, telephone calls and frequent correspondence could serve as constant reminders that the young person is truly loved and missed by *both* parents.

REMARRIAGE

Many youngsters secretly hope that their parents will someday be reconciled. When the announcement comes that "father will be remarried" and "to some *other* woman!" the offspring may receive a stunning blow. They now know that their real mother and father will never bridge the gap and heal the breach.

Once again, there could be a feeling of rejection. "How dare he fall in love with someone else? I thought he loved me. If he wanted to marry, why not my mommy? Then we could all be together again."

Both mother and father must again assist the children to grow out of their imaginative fancy. "When we were divorced, our decision was final. It was and is still better for us to live separately. Daddy's being married does not change our future. We both love you, and even though your father has a new wife he will still come to visit with you." Never equate remarriage with abandonment.

The offspring may make a fast play for the affection of another male as a replacement for the father who is "leaving" to be married. He may ask the mother: "Will you find me another father?" The answer again must be truthful. "I don't know about the future. Someday I may be married. But not because your daddy has a new wife." In other words, the mother's possible remarriage is not as a substitute or punishment for the father's actions. Divorced people also fall in love, and find happiness with their new spouses.

If the mother remarries, and the children remain with her, they may at first be hostile toward the new man in the house. He is the interloper, the intruder. He is even sleeping in the same bed with the mother! In their eyes, the mother's actions may seem disloyal and traitorous both to their father and to them. Before, they were almost the totality of the mother's life; now they have to "share" her. But children must understand that people love in different ways. "I love you but I can also love my new husband. One does not take away from the other. Do you remember when we sat on the rocks and watched the ocean and how surprised you were that the waves kept coming and the ocean never ran dry. So it is with affection. Love is the only thing in the world that multiplies by division. The more you give of it, the more there is." You will discover that even though there may be moments of resentment and open rebellion toward the new husband, there may also develop, in time, tenderness and dependence.

(Jetse Sprey relates in detail the various opinions current in sociological thought regarding the potential harm to children resulting from remarriage.)

HELPING CHILDREN OF DIVORCE

Most important is that the mother and father help the youngsters to face reality without loss of security. Answer their questions with the most appropriate factual responses. The task is not to hide unpleasant truths, but step by step, to help them face authentic events with knowledge rather than fanciful imagination.

Speak with them, not to them. They need to talk, not just to be talked to. Converse in such a way as to encourage their ability to think, digest, decide, and choose what is significant. In the words of the psychiatrist Dr. Viktor Frankl, "We can shoulder any suffering as long as we can see a meaning in it."

Listen to the nature of the children's real concerns. The deeper question may not appear at first. Each of us, whether child or adult, lives in a different perceptual world; we see and construct our pictures of the universe in terms of our own needs and emotional experiences. The point is that we must be careful to realize that each youngster will have his own unique way of viewing, and framing his view of, the world about him.

One of the great gifts that you can give your children at this time is the right to feel. Aid them to discover themselves. Never turn away from their thoughts or brand them as "insignificant" or "childish." Allow the antipathy, resentment, and guilt to wither in the sunlight rather than attempt to pull them out by the roots by condemning the children for their real emotions.

In guiding children of divorce toward a more meaningful future, your aim is both to understand their needs and also to find healthy ways of meeting them. Remember, they are still children. Youngsters expected to perform like adults may feel that they have now replaced the absent parent. Physical intimacy such as sharing a bedroom should be tactfully avoided. Seductive and sexually stimulating situations bring embarrassment and guilt.

Don't try to "make up" to them by overindulgence. This would obliterate their desire to bend their efforts toward achievement and deprive them of attaining satisfactions in their own endeavors. Nor should they be subject to punitiveness—the venting of your own recurring personal hostility. They should never be treated as an unwanted burden, a nuisance and source of trouble. They should receive the privilege of growing up and occasionally being naughty and mischievous. Parents should not be too demanding nor too permissive. The object is balance.

Aid them to get out of themselves. Perhaps they might become more active in a youth group or club. Just as you need release from your tensions, so do they need relaxation outside of the family circle.

You will get discouraged. At best, it is not easy to raise youngsters. Just remember, everyone at times becomes depressed. Know that many of the perplexities of the child in a one-parent family are the same as those of children with two parents, only accentuated a little more. Just as you should not demand too much from the offspring, so do not create unrealistic requirements for yourself. Goals should be flexible. Take one day at a time. Accept what little you can do at the moment, even as you strive to accomplish a little more in the future. If you reject yourself as a failure, you will only create a more difficult environment for the children.

Ultimately, you can only bring alive for your children an outlook on life which is authentic for you. It is only as you now search and find answers for yourself that you may help your offspring to search and find answers for themselves. This will demand your best wisdom, your most loving efforts.

Earl A. Grollman

Just as there are no two children alike, there are no two divorces alike. Each separation will have a special and unique meaning.

Yet, though each person is different from the other, there are certain likenesses among groups. Sociology is the scientific study of human interaction. Human behavior is social behavior in that it involves taking other individuals into account.

Dr. Jetse Sprey gives an overview into the many forms of family disorganization. His research inquires systematically into a large aggregate of cases to discern common patterns of adjustment.

A native of Arnhem, Netherlands, Jetse Sprey was educated both in Europe and the United States, receiving his doctorate in sociology at Yale University. He has taught at Franklin and Marshall College in Pennsylvania and is presently Associate Professor of Sociology at Case Western Reserve University in Cleveland, Ohio. Dr. Sprey's special field of interest is the family as adapted to the structural arrangements of society. In this chapter, he describes the social concerns of children in divorce.

CHILDREN IN DIVORCE: AN OVERVIEW

BY *Jetse Sprey*

SOCIOLOGICALLY SPEAKING, divorce—the dissolution of a valid marriage in a court of law—must be considered a process rather than a distinct event. Its courtroom stage is preceded by a more or less extended period of marital maladjustment, and is followed by a sequel which lasts as long as both former partners are alive. For the law may declare married individuals single again, or in the case of an annulment make believe that a marriage never existed, but it cannot alter the social fact that those involved will remain ex-husbands and ex-wives for the rest of their lives. These are new social roles that have to be learned by trial and error, and occasionally at the cost of personal distress. Because, ironically in our society with its high divorce rate, most marital counseling is still aimed at preventing divorce rather than learning to cope with it.

In the case of a childless marriage, especially when no alimony is paid, former spouses may literally disappear from each other's lives. This is difficult, if not impossible, when children are involved. Legally the child's custody is never unalterably settled, and furthermore, visitation rights, financial arrangements, and the like, will keep such a marriage unbroken long after its legal dissolution. Matters of this nature can, however, be arranged and when necessary enforced by the court. But this is not true for the common identity and mutual loyalty between parents and their children that was established before—and continues after—the marital breakup. It was noted that our culture does provide new roles for the formerly married, while the institution of remarriage makes a new start possible for most of them. No such provisions are available to structure the status of parenthood in the divorce procedure. One cannot be an ex-parent nor an ex-child in our society.

Parents and children participate jointly in the divorce process; they have no choice in the matter. Their relationship will continue after the marriage of which they were all a part has been legally dissolved. What *has* been changed then is the social and legal structure of their common identity. It is the aim of this chapter to pay special attention to the participation of children in the divorce process, and to sketch some of the ways in which it may affect their lives. Our perspective is sociological, that is, focuses upon the many individual dramas of family dissolution as they occur in a social setting. It is assumed that much of the well-being of the individual actors, young and old, will depend upon the clarity, rationality, and sensibility of the social rules and values that define the social stage on which their individual drama is enacted.

In view of the above, a number of issues will be raised and discussed below. The treatment must by necessity be brief. The aim is more to raise questions than to provide the answers. First, to understand what exactly children—and adults—are participating in, the legal and the social structure of divorce in our society must both be described. Then, some factual information—how many divorces involve children, how does the presence of children seem to affect the divorce trend, what are the relationships between these factors—must be presented. Next is the issue of the impact of divorce on children. Lastly, attention will be paid to the reaction of children to the remarriage of their parents.

THE LEGAL SETTING

Marriage is a contract to be terminated by death or in a court of law. Thus both divorce and annulment—a legal declaration that no valid marriage ever existed—are matters of civil law. However, a simple, straightforward agreement by a couple to divorce is against legal policy. Instead, one of the spouses, usually the wife, sues for divorce using a legal ground available in the state in which the action takes place. The divorce procedure is a contest incorporating an innocent and a guilty party. If the guilt is proven to the satisfaction of the court the defendant is "punished" by the dissolution of the marriage. In view of the fact that most divorces go uncontested and reflect a mutual desire of both spouses to quit an unsatisfactory relationship, this procedure is remarkably unrealistic. Moreover, it has a number of negative social and psychological consequences.

Despite the fact that most intelligent people realize that in a strained marital relationship neither spouse is either completely guilty or innocent, the public tendency to consider each marital breakup within a guilty-innocent context is still widespread, and is continuously reinforced by our legal procedure. Furthermore, the enforced legal contest, with its formal accusations, mutually reestablished distrust, and possible judicial punishment in the form of alimony and custody decisions, is hardly conducive toward the maintenance of a civil and rational relationship between the former spouses. Such an attitude is badly needed if mutual arrangements about the future of the children have to be arrived at.

It is in this type of situation that the children are caught. Some of the most vicious courtroom battles are fought over their custody. But even in those many instances where the matters of custody and financial support have been settled out of court, the children's fate and future well-being are often determined in an atmosphere of mutual recrimination, and through bargaining rather than genuine cooperation.[1] Again, the insidious effects of the contest structure are apparent. Custody of the children, visitation rights for the non-custodial parent may be used as levers in demands for more financial support or measured against other extraneous issues. Finally, it is not unusual for one spouse to use its legal power over the children simply as a way of getting back at the other one.

The court is supposed to act in behalf of the children, but is not directly involved in the previously arranged settlements. In those cases where the final decision is up to him, the judge often has only his own personal views and biases to guide him in a decision which may determine the fate of the children in question. Some courts have established special procedures to provide a maximum of knowledge and experience in dealing with such cases, but these are exceptions rather than the rule.[2] To aggravate matters, the decision regarding child custody may be affected by the legal make-believe of the divorce proceedings. Courts seem reluctant to grant custody to a "guilty" party. This despite the fact that pleading guilty in a divorce suit seems hardly a basis for the evaluation of the quality of parenthood. What *is* happening in such cases is that the future of the children is ranked second to the irrational wish to punish the guilty parent by denying him, or her, custody over the children.

THE SOCIAL NATURE OF DIVORCE

Paradoxically, divorce is very much a part of marriage. Apart from the truism that to get a divorce one needs to be married first, it is not, as many people feel, merely an event which destroys a given marriage. On the contrary, the way in which divorce is defined in our culture, the degree to which it is socially accepted, and even the individual motivations that drive so many married couples toward it, reflect the way we expect our institutions of marriage and the family to be. So as to understand some of the major consequences of divorce for those involved—parents and children —we must look at the nature of marriage and the family.

The American family system is a so-called *multilineal* and *conjugal* one. It is also characterized by predominantly *neolocal* living arrangements. In a multilineal system, a married couple's children are considered related to both sides of the family (despite our tradition that the children assume the father's surname). This means that in our society neither set of relatives has preferential power over them.

Our system is conjugal in the sense that the so-called nuclear family—parents and children—is of the most basic importance in our kinship system. This is not to say that other relatives are totally ignored; far from it. It does mean, however, that they have little formal decision-making power left. Finally, as apparent from each successive population census, it is becoming increasingly common for newly married couples to live on their own.

The relevance of all this for the understanding of divorce and its impact upon children was noted years ago by Kingsley Davis.[3] He pointed out that in most non-Western societies problems of child custody do not exist. In a so-called patrilineal kinship system the children are members of the father's kin group only, in a matrilineal system of the mother's only. In a situation of family dissolution the fate of the children is thus settled at the outset. They remain members of their own kin group and are its responsibility.

Davis stresses another important factor: the small and intimate nature of our modern conjugal family. On the average, American households are small. Increasingly they contain only members of one nuclear family. The relationship between the parents and the children is, predictably, a deeply personal one. Children are assumed to love and respect both parents equally. There is no place to hide in the modern family. Under such conditions children, especially older ones, can be expected to participate intensely in the divorce process.

It is argued here that the question of custody, as seen from the child's angle—as it should be—is, in abstracto at least, unsolvable. In asking the child to state which parent he prefers he is asked to evaluate something that he has been taught not to rank before: the loyalty and love for either parent. In asking children to choose between their parents, and the latter to state a preference for individual children, one of the most basic of our cultural prescriptions about the nature of family identity is being violated. No wonder that we find this question to pose an awful dilemma for those involved. Case materials from courtroom files, lawyers, and other qualified observers of our divorce proceedings[4] amply illustrate this point.

We have created a family system in our society in which a general rule about the future of the children of divorce is virtually impossible. No laws or moral principles can possibly be devised to solve our problems. On the contrary, the one and only solution seems to lie in a set of guidelines which incorporate a maximum of flexibility, and from which any considerations other than the well-being of the children in question, that is, those involved in one specific case, are totally excluded.

THE STATISTICAL PICTURE

Approximately four hundred thousand marriages end in divorce or annulment each year in this country.[5] While the divorce rate is leveling off, the actual number granted is steadily increasing due to the still rising rate of marriage. More children seem to be involved each successive year. Since most divorces are granted during the first seven years of the marriage, many of these children are quite young. Table I provides a summary of this trend.

TABLE I. *Estimated Number of Children Involved in Divorces and Annulments: U.S. 1955–64*

Year	All Divorces and Annulments	Estimated Number of Children	Average Number per Divorce	Rate per 1,000 Children in Pop.
1955	377,000	347,000	.92	6.3
1960	393,000	463,000	1.18	7.2
1964	450,000	634,000	1.41	9.0

Source: "Vital Statistics of the United States," 1964, Vol. III, *Marriage and Divorce,* Table 2–9.

It seems that the average number of children per divorce is steadily increasing, while their proportion in our total population is also on the rise. There could be a number of reasons for this phenomenon. The belief that one should continue a bad marriage for the sake of the children may be on its way out. It is also possible, however, that more couples resort to the conception of children to bolster a shaky relationship. Or the data may merely reflect a tendency for larger families to get divorces more often than in the past. None of these suggestions provides more than a guess, and among students of divorce opinions differ greatly.

To round out the statistical picture a further factor, that of the duration of the marriage at the time of dissolution, can be added. Table II shows that 66.2 per cent of the

TABLE II. *Divorces and Annulments by Duration of Marriage and Number of Minor Children Reported, in Percentages, U.S. 1964*

| Duration of Marriage | Number of Children Reported | | | | | |
	None	1	2	3+	Not Known	Totals
1–4 yrs.	49.4	30.0	10.3	3.2	7.0	100.0
5–9 yrs.	24.9	21.3	25.1	22.6	6.1	100.0
10–14 yrs.	20.4	14.5	21.5	37.2	6.3	100.0
15 yrs. or more	31.7	17.0	17.5	33.9	7.3	100.0
Not Known	7.1	5.3	3.0	4.1	80.5	100.0
All	33.8	21.8	16.8	18.0	9.7	100.0

Source: "Vital Statistics of the United States," 1964, Vol. III, *Marriage and Divorce,* Table 2–19.

divorces in the 1964 Census sample include children under 18 years of age. In 1960 this figure was estimated to be 56.7 per cent. Apparently the proportion of divorcing fami-

lies with children is increasing. This offers one explanation
for the trend reflected in our first table.

It is not too surprising to see that marriages of a relatively short duration—less than five years—are at the time
of divorce more likely to be childless than those in other
categories. About half of these do include children, however, in most cases only one. The normal procreative
sequence in many of such marriages has either been fore-
stalled or interrupted by the onset of marital problems. In
the second category, marriages that lasted between five and
ten years, we find a different picture. About one-fourth are
childless, but no specific family size dominates the field.
Here too, however, some marriages probably dissolved before the intended family size was reached. This assumption
is supported by the figures for the last two categories, all of
which lasted a minimum of ten years. In both cases approximately one-third of the couples have at least three children.
The proportion of childless divorces remains fairly constant.
The slight increase in the fifteen years and up category may
be due to the fact that the census measures childless divorces
as those without the presence of minor children.

The question remains: what does all this mean? For one,
the limited data show that the exact nature of the association
between the presence of children, the duration of marriages,
and the tendency of the latter to break up, is far from clear.
Jacobson, in probably the most comprehensive, but somewhat dated, statistical treatment of marriage and divorce
attempted to get closer to the causative factors at work by
comparing the divorce rates for existing marriages with and
without children.[6] Each category was thus considered a distinct population, so to speak. He concluded that the "differential in the divorce rate between childless couples and
those with children is not uniform throughout married
life." Divorce turned out to be more frequent among those

without children in the early years of marriage, but the differential diminished rapidly thereafter. After the thirtieth year of marriage it disappeared completely. This is in accord with the data shown above. Apparently a variety of selective factors operate: in some marriages problems arise almost immediately; some of these break up subsequently, almost half of them without children, fortunately. In and by itself being childless is, however, no guarantee for, or against, anything. We see childless marriages dissolve after ten or fifteen years. In some of these the absence of children may be a contributing factor, in others not. The same seems to hold for the presence of offspring. Marriages break up all through the procreative and child-rearing stages of the family life cycle. Unions of longer duration are, as a category, more likely to have three or more children at the time of their dissolution than one or two. This may well indicate that not infrequently marital disharmony either did not preclude procreation or manifested itself after the birth of at least some of the children. Furthermore, these marriages were not continued for the sake of the children, at least not indefinitely. One is inclined to conclude that in answer to the question; what exactly are the effects of the presence or absence of children upon the divorce process, the best answer would be: that depends.

THE IMPACT OF DIVORCE ON CHILDREN

The next issue to be dealt with is the one doubtless responsible for much of the social concern aimed at divorce: its impact on children. The problem has received attention from professionals of many disciplines. Many answers have been given, many solutions offered. However, many different questions have been asked also. This makes the evaluation of the answers often quite difficult. We must, therefore, start out by specifying what questions must be raised.

Assuming the simple fact that, all things being equal, divorce may be expected to be a traumatic experience for children, one might ask: what exactly is the causal agent of the trauma? Is it the prelude of marital disharmony? The stresses and strains of the courtroom contest? The necessity to continue life in an incomplete family? Or all of these? It seems realistic to consider each of these relevant, but their impact is likely to vary greatly under different conditions.

Many factors have been found to affect the consequences of divorce. Relevant are: ages, number, and sex of the children; the duration of the marriage; the age of the parents; and social variables such as race, religious affiliation, socio-economic class position, residence, and nationality.[7] The diversity of relevant factors is so large, their possible combinations so numerous, that the query: what is the impact of divorce on children? becomes analogous to: what is the color of birds? It is, therefore, not too startling to find at least one sociologist comment that "children of divorce cannot be treated as a homogeneous group."[8] This statement was made in conclusion to a study about the effect of divorce on children, in which it was found that its impact occurred in a number of ways, depending on such factors as the age of the child at the time of the divorce and how it perceived the home situation before it learned about the pending breakup.

A similar view is held by Rosenberg, who investigated the consequences of divorce, and other forms of family dissolution, for the emotional stability of adolescents.[9] He reports that the emotional reactions of children depended "on who had been divorced . . . on when they divorced . . . and, on what happened after they were divorced." And, more specifically, on the parents' religion: Catholicism or Jewishness seemed to have a clear negative effect, Protestantism had little or no effect. The mother's age at the time of breakup also mattered: in the case of young mothers there was a clear negative effect, not so if the mother was older. Rosenberg suggests a number of explanatory factors to account for his findings, respectively: the differential attitudes among religious groups toward divorce, and the degree to which the remaining parent is able to cope with the problems of maintaining a family.[10]

It lies beyond the scope of this chapter to attempt a decisive inquiry into the exact nature of the complex relationships between the numerous conditions which may, or may not, influence the divorce process and its consequences for the children participating in it. Any statement of this nature would at the present state of our empirical knowledge be far from complete and only be presumptuous. The foregoing data were presented in order to stress the great importance and complexity of those situational factors which form the social and psychological setting for each individual divorce action.

Research about the effects of divorce on children has been directed toward two general foci: the potential emotional damage to the offspring, and such behavioral consequences as incidence of delinquency, school performance, and the like. The two categories are not independent of one another, the distinction is therefore more descriptive than analytical.

One of the most quoted studies in the behavioral category is that by the Gluecks.[11] In a carefully designed survey the authors found that separation, widowhood, and divorce were more likely to characterize the families of delinquents than those of nondelinquents. The relationship held even after social class was statistically controlled. This type of finding is, of course, in itself not too surprising. One would hardly expect family dissolution to be associated with improvement in conduct, especially when comparing broken and intact families as total categories. General comparisons between families broken by divorce and intact ones are

therefore not too meaningful. More enlightening are comparisons between different categories of divorced families—
such as conducted by Rosenberg, for example—or between
divorced families and intact but unhappy families.

A number of studies indicate that when children from
intact homes are compared with ones from incomplete families, the former show a somewhat better emotional adjustment.[12] Other research findings contradict such conclusions,
though. One of the most thorough investigations of mental
health, the Midtown Manhattan study,[13] showed that, on
the average, persons who had been raised in broken homes
had only a slightly higher risk of emotional disturbance
than those from unbroken ones. The difference disappeared
completely for those of a higher socio-economic background.
Rosenberg's guarded conclusions were mentioned earlier.
Goode, in an important study of the post-divorce adjustment
of formerly married women,[14] fails to find any conclusive
evidence of a general negative effect on children. In fact, his
evidence seems to point in the opposite direction.

Nye and Landis, in two independent surveys, compared
children from homes broken by divorce with those living in
intact, but unhappy, ones. Nye found children from broken
homes to do better every time. They showed less psychosomatic illness, less delinquency, and better relationships
with parents than children from intact unhappy households.
Furthermore, the two groups did not differ significantly with
regard to adjustment in school or church.[15]

Landis provides similar findings. He concludes that while
the two groups of children exhibit many personality simi-
larities, those from the unhappy complete families made the
worse showing.[16]

Finally, a more recent study by Burchinal lends additional support to the above two.[17] He investigated the effect of divorce upon school relationships and personality

adjustment of adolescents, while holding the factor of socio-economic class constant. His main conclusion was that adolescents from divorced families appeared no worse off than their classmates from intact ones.

CHILDREN AND PARENTAL REMARRIAGE

Most divorced people remarry. As a matter of fact, they are more likely to do so than either single or widowed individuals of the same ages. Jacobson reports that men who divorced in their twenties were usually remarried in less than two years, while the women in this category tended to marry again within three.[18] Women with children seemed to remarry as quickly as those without.

The question; how does remarriage, especially that of the custodial parent, affect the children, is thus a relevant one. Looking at remarriage as a process, two issues warrant our attention. Firstly, how do children react to a new courtship of the remaining parent? Secondly, what are the consequences of living with a stepparent?

On the first point, the part taken by the children in the courtship of a divorced parent, little reliable information is available. Most data are of an ex post facto, that is, "after the fact," nature. They are recorded after the new marriage is in existence. Such information is, of course, useful but may be colored by wishful thinking of the parent in question, or by the subsequent course of events in the new family.

Some insight can be gained from the works of William Goode, Louise Despert, and Morton Hunt. Goode's *Women in Divorce* provides statistical data. He noticed that the number of children and the attitude of the mother toward them tended to influence the speed with which the latter remarried. "It would appear that the mothers who gave more attention to their children would fail to get remarried."[19] On the other hand, those with more children were, as a category, more likely to remarry soon. He suggests that the latter may organize their "remarriage activities" better than those with fewer children.

It is clear that other explanations about these seemingly contradictory data can be formulated. Mothers with large families may, for example, lower their standards in order to find a new spouse. Whatever explanation we come up with, however, it seems that children, in one way or other, may have to pay a price if their mother intends to remarry soon and organizes her life accordingly.

Case materials presented in Hunt's and Despert's books support this idea.[20] From Morton Hunt's *The World of the Formerly Married*—an unusually honest book—one receives the distinct impression that children frequently are seen as a nuisance to the divorced parent engaged in a new courtship. The latter, often absorbed in his, or her, own problems, tends to rationalize the pursuit of a new partner as an attempt to first and foremost find a new parent for the children. Children, however, sometimes do not see it this way.

Apart from this, and other more obvious problems such as the difficulty of explaining the desire to remarry, the loyalty of the child to the absent parent, and so forth, other situations which may require great communicative skills and mutual understanding are likely to arise. Hunt, for example, mentions the fact that many divorced individuals, men and women alike, tend to engage in sexual relationships with potential new spouses, or with steady dating partners. How does one explain this to one's children? Can a divorced woman carry on an affair while at the same time attempting to enforce the chastity of a teenage daughter? Or, if she denies herself such a relationship for the sake of the children, will she blame the latter? One thing becomes quite clear from a perusal of the works of Despert, Hunt, and others, and that is that the road toward remarriage has to be traveled by both parent and children. Frequently, it is a hard one.

On the fate of the stepchild in a new family a great deal of literature is available. Conclusions, and findings, are again far from unanimous. It is unfortunate that occasionally the issue of the desirability of remarriage per se and that of its effect upon children tend to be confused. Many individuals—social scientists and laymen alike—feel that from a societal perspective remarriage of single parents is highly desirable. This judgment reflects to some extent the fact that the so-called incomplete family has never become a culturally accepted feature in our society. At best, it is considered a temporary condition. It is felt that, all things being equal, parents should have partners, and children two parents. Ideally, thus, the remarriage of a single parent is considered to be beneficial by definition. This means that in cases where problems arise, individuals, rather than the mere fact of the remarriage itself, are singled out for blame.

In view of the foregoing, a brief mention of some of the major research findings on the topic in question is warranted. Rosenberg, in the earlier quoted study, found that children whose mothers remarried seemed more disturbed than those whose mothers remained single. This negative effect was especially strong for older children.[21] Langner and Michael, in the Manhattan project,[22] observed that the remarriage of the remaining parent appeared associated with a clear increase in emotional disturbances, especially if the parent of the same sex remarried. Bowerman flatly states that "homes involving step-relationships proved more likely to have stress, ambivalence, and low cohesiveness than did normal homes," while "the presence of stepparents in the home affected also the adjustment of the children to the natural parents, usually somewhat diminishing the level of adjustment."[23]

In contrast, Jessie Bernard in her study of remarriage arrives at the conclusion that "remarriage is not necessarily harmful to the children."[24] She gives three reasons in support of her conclusion: the favorable attitude of most children toward remarriage, the fact that the new parent may prove to be a salvaging force, and, finally, a "reservoir of resiliency" in the human condition that makes it possible for people to adjust themselves to the blows of life. Bernard's optimism seems shared by Morton Hunt, who feels that remarriage moderates the effect of divorce on children, but his observations seem, at careful scrutiny, to reflect wishful thinking rather than solid data. A conclusion by Goode does support Bernard's views somewhat, however. He mentions that almost all remarried mothers in his sample did feel that the lives of their children had improved after the divorce.[25] It is not clear, however, what exactly serves as basis for comparison here: the preceding unhappy marriage or the subsequent period of single parenthood.

In view of the fact that most divorced parents eventually *do* remarry, and in light of the inherent rationality of the premise that most children may be better off with two parents than one, the above findings warrant our full attention. The research literature on the stepchild and his family is growing, while its image is abundantly represented in our literature and folklore. The latter may serve as a reminder that the plight of the stepchild was recognized well before the birth of the social sciences.

On the whole, the verdict still seems a negative one. The "reservoir of resilience" so hopefully invoked by Jessie Bernard all too frequently runs dry in the face of the strains and stresses of the real world. On the other hand, the research quoted above is still scattered and far from complete in coverage. The design of Landis, Nye, and Burchinal has not been duplicated in the area of remarriage; no systematic comparison has been made between the situation of the step-child and his contemporary in an unhappy intact family, or even between the former and children living in unhappy incomplete households. Until such research has been completed and its findings are available, we will have to withhold final judgment.

It seems justified to assume that the problems of the stepfamily often originate before the actual marriage ceremony. As pointed out above, little is known about the courtship process of the divorced parent, but its cultural ambiguity and lack of definition is reflected in the total lack of guidelines, goals, and meanings designed to help people deal with such a situation. This is in glaring contrast to the ever growing volume of counseling and guidance literature designed to facilitate the problems of the first, premarital, mate selection, and courtship stages of the family cycle.

IN CONCLUSION

As shown in the foregoing, the proportion of divorces involving children is steadily increasing, as is the proportion and absolute number of children of divorce among our total population. Furthermore, no clearcut statistical relationship between the absence or presence of children and the tendency of families to end in divorce or annulment can be established. Some factors, especially the duration of marriage, do differentiate to some degree in *combination* with the presence of children, but what exactly is causing what is impossible to state for certain.

In much the same way many answers given with regard to the impact of divorce on children seem to beg their own questions. Beyond the simplistic observation that divorce,

preceded by a period of marital maladjustment can, all
things being equal, be hardly expected to benefit the children, one is confronted with a host of complex relationships
which, at our present state of empirical knowledge, still
seem to defy generalization and systematization. What
research *is* available indicates that first and foremost all judg-
ments about the effect of divorce on children depend essentially upon one's standards of comparison. As a category,
children in homes broken by divorce seem to do better than
those in unhappy intact households. On the other hand, the
differences *within* the category "children of divorce" are so
large, and vary so much in relation to many social and psychological factors, that some sociologists tend to reject the
category as meaningless for explanatory purposes.

Despite all this, some general observations—of a non-
statistical nature—about the participation of children in
our current divorce process can be made. They will provide
us with a framework in which the increasing amount of
factual information, be it of psychological, sociological, or
strictly personal nature, can be interpreted, and perhaps better understood.

First of all, the dilemma connected with the future of the
children of divorce is essentially a result of the way in which
we ourselves, through our culture, have come to define our
institutions of marriage and the family. In view of the individualistic, equalitarian, and intimate nature of our modern family, the problem of what to do with the children in
case of a breakup cannot be solved in a general, standard-
ized way. Under these conditions the one and only way to
avoid such a dilemma is not to have any children at all, or to
wait till one is absolutely certain that the marriage in question is going to work out. Unfortunately our data show that
exactly the opposite seems to occur.

Then there is the issue of the remarriage of the divorced

parents, in particular the one—usually the mother—with whom the children reside. Despite the fact that theoretically remarriage seems an excellent solution to the problems of the incomplete family resulting from divorce, most available research findings provide a negative verdict about its merits for the children. Again, we find great differences, older children seem to suffer more than the very young ones, while the sex of the child and that of the remarrying parent is also of importance.

The question is, why? Why is it that children in broken homes do not welcome a new parent with open arms and again settle gladly within the security and normalcy of a new and presumably happy family? The fact that we cannot answer this question, reflects more than anything else our basic ignorance about the way children participate in the divorce process. For this reason, this chapter as a whole, and the following final sentences in particular, are intended as an attempt to respond to this specific query.

It is suggested, then, that parents, counselors, judges, and other participating adults tend to underestimate the loyalty of children to both parents and fail to grasp the meaning of a family identity for them. It seems indicative of the arrogance and insensitivity of the adult world that it is still felt by many that a child's family world can be dissolved by a court decision, that a court can decide who is to be the relevant parent in its future life. It was pointed out above that the legal dissolution of a marriage is far from "final" for many adults involved; this is even more so for the children. It seems, therefore, that whether or not children will adjust to the remarriage of the custodial parent will depend on what took place before the divorce, and during the subsequent period of single-parenthood. Case materials provided by Despert, Plant, and many others not mentioned in this chapter, indicate that often children prefer one parent over the other. If the child is in the custody of the favored parent, remarriage may be a reasonably safe bet.

As stressed above, children are caught in the divorce process involuntarily, and frequently feel acutely aware of their inability to do anything about it. The same is true for the remarriage of a parent. From the viewpoint of the children remarriage as an *event* may well be of equal, if not greater, importance than the personality traits or economic status of the new parent. In contrast, it is in all likelihood the latter factors which are most important to the remarrying parent in question. A new father is not just a nice man, with perhaps a good income, but someone who is going to occupy the father role with all its associated expectations, and meanings, in that small and intimate world that we call the family. Impressions received from Hunt's and Goode's reports about the courtship and remarriage of the remaining parent indicate that this awareness, from the side of the parent, is all too often lacking. As a matter of fact, the reading of such sources leaves one with the feeling that it is surprising that so many stepfamilies do work out well. When this occurs, it must be credited in many cases to the resilience and understanding of the children rather than the wisdom of the adults.

Before you can explain questions of separation and divorce, you must first understand the age ability of the child to understand these thoughts. The research of Piaget and others highlights the fact that at each stage of development the youngster has a characteristic way of seeing the world and explaining it to himself.

Dr. Evelyn Goodenough Pitcher has dedicated her life to the understanding of young children. She is Chairman of the Eliot-Pearson Department of Child Study at Tufts University and a consultant to the Department of Health, Education and Welfare, Children's Bureau.

Professor Pitcher received her Ph.D. degree at Yale and LL.D. at New England College. She has both authored and edited numerous books, including Children Tell Stories: An Analysis of Fantasy, The Guidance Nursery School, *and* Helping Young Children Learn. *Her theme in explaining divorce to young children is that the effects must be understood in terms of the youngster's total life experience.*

EXPLAINING DIVORCE TO YOUNG CHILDREN

BY *Evelyn Goodenough Pitcher*

THE SUBJECT OF DIVORCE is one which is fraught with emotions for those adults contemplating it. The natural and crucial question which parents ask is, "How can we explain this to our children in such a way that their suffering will be minimal?" Handling such a problem is a difficult and complex task because one needs to consider so many variables, especially when dealing with the young child. To recognize what divorce means to the young child, one must explore what the family unit means, and what the subsequent loss of an integral part of such a unit means to the child.

One is further encumbered by the fact that the young child is limited in his understanding of verbal explanations because of his limited vocabulary and his need for concrete experiences before he can assimilate an abstract idea. Also, many parents have not clarified in their own minds their motivations for getting a divorce and thus cannot put their feelings into words for themselves, let alone into simple explanations for their children.

Those parents facing the problem of explaining divorce to young children from two to five years of age could be enlightened by reading sections of a book similar to this one, *Explaining Death to Children*.[1] At once the analogies between the two experiences are apparent: both threaten personal security, since the dependent child looks primarily to his parents for protection, and death and divorce could threaten the solidarity of his world. The very words, *death, divorce,* are abstract, mysterious—foreign to the life-experience of the young child. In family situations involving death or divorce the young child may suffer not only feelings of loss, but irrational feelings of guilt, which I will discuss later.

It is difficult to evaluate which experience would be more traumatic. Needless to say, behavior of parents is directly related to the child's adaptation to death or divorce. The child needs somehow the sharing of the parents' experience, with parents realizing that words won't make the difference, that feelings are what you must watch out for. Therefore emotions of deep despair and anxiety, or of anger and hostility, the child could feel but not constructively interpret.

The almost inevitable hostilities between parents before, during, and after divorce do not promote the child's well-being.[2] The young child learns basic values and feelings from his parents. Ideally such values include love and respect, tolerance, freedom, and discipline, a sense of humor, curiosity, and creativity. The transmission of such values could be jeopardized if parents' emotions are expended on hate and disrespect, intolerance, coercion, unhappiness, and inflexible views of the world. To be sure, many parents say it is not the divorce, but the imposed continuation of a hateful marriage that nourishes negative values. That may be true. I feel, however, that parents must be acutely and especially aware of their feelings and values when they embark upon their divorce, for the age of infancy to five seems to be unusually sensitive to assimilating foundations for feeling and being. Can parents who are separating genuinely reassure the child that they are sorry this had to happen? Can they share the child's inevitable grief, and identify with and support the child's continuing affection for the other parent? Both would be easy in the case of death, but much more difficult in the case of divorce.

In the last analysis, perhaps the emotions involved with death are easier to assimilate than those generated by divorce. Death is a human predicament; as soon as a person is born, each day involves for each person the possible ceasing of his life. The emergence of religion in every society is intimately related to every man's desire to understand what is not understandable, and to deny the extinction of his own being and of those he loves. In many ways acceptance and concern for death occupy every person's life, as he provides for his property, cares for his health, formulates his goals and philosophy for living. Therefore, a young child's experiencing death means that, at an early age, he has prematurely come to grips with something everyone must face. Rituals, society, religion, literature, music—much of the beautifully creative productions of man have come from those who contemplate death and share their feelings. So the child, although he may be hurt, and anxious and confused, has a vast potential healing reservoir as he becomes increasingly able to share the anguish and healings of his fellow men.

Divorce, although it is increasingly practiced in our society, is not a universal predicament. There has been progress in the understanding of human relations, so that the dissolving of hostile unions has become more commonplace, yet to many people divorce still carries stigma. It breaks a contract made with church and state; it reveals undesirable personal incompatibility; it threatens the strength of the nuclear family, the chief unit of our social structure.

Therefore, the young child whose parents divorce is threatened with a loss similar to that of death, without the possible healing involved in sharing a universal experience. To be sure, society may pity him and seek to help him. But all too often such pity is accompanied by a one-sided support of one parent against the other. And the bountiful neighbor all too often can attempt to help the child mainly to denigrate one of his parents.

Thus far I have not directed specific remarks toward just how parents explain divorce to a young child, the assignment of this chapter. I have not done so because, as already said, the mechanics, the words of explanation are of secondary importance. The young child does not usually understand words as such unless he has built up many concrete experiences to make these words meaningful. It is not likely that this would have ordinarily happened with regard to divorce. Parents announcing, "we are going to get a divorce," might with equal ambiguity announce, "we are going to Zanzibar," or "we're about to liquidate our capital," so far as the child's understanding is concerned. There are many studies and illustrations of a young child's inability to understand abstract words, and of his confusions about what adults take for granted.[3] Parents who have no loving regard for one another must deal with the task of presenting personal emotions and feelings that are constructive and concrete. Ideally, they should show continued support and love for the child, and display their ability to communicate with one another as friends.

Since words like divorce or separation are so meaningless to a young child, it seems to me wise for parents not to discuss such an impending event in the presence of the child until they themselves have come to grips with all the practical arrangements. If it is possible to communicate these arrangements with friends and relatives in advance, to assure them this is the parents' mutual intent, it could help subsequent contacts the child has with people outside the family. When a decision and arrangements have been fully thought out, parents together might deal with each child in the family separately for the appropriate communication, since each age and each personality will call for a somewhat different approach. The formal calling of the clan for a group announcement would seem to me to carry uncontrollable hazards.

As far as possible, parents should try to keep an excess of emotion from their voices, their attitudes, their feelings, when they tell the child, not once but many times, that, "Daddy and Mommy have decided not to live together in the same house. Daddy and Mommy will not be married anymore; they will be divorced. We are sorry this has to be the way, but Mommy and Daddy think this is best for everyone."

It seems advisable to use the words marriage and divorce in these situations, with the full realization they may not mean anything to the child initially. The child will soon hear them from others. As he repeatedly hears the words, he will attach meanings to them. Parents must be prepared not only to talk, but to get the child to talk, and express feelings. Soon he will question, "Why?" Much cannot be said of an expository nature, but I prefer not saying, "Your father (mother) and I don't love one another anymore." I prefer, "Your father (mother) and I decided we did not want to be married anymore." My concern is that the child, who will often hear that he is loved (but not married) may worry if some caprice will mean he also may not be loved anymore.

In any case, "not married" and "divorced" is the first essential message to convey. At the same time, the child needs to have some emotional assurance that the father and mother will both continue to care for him and love him, and that the father and mother will carry on in an emotional respect for one another. Usually the child needs also to know where he will stay. "You will live in Mommy's house, this same house, because Daddy cannot stay at home. He needs to go to work to make money for the things we need. He will show you his new house soon." A similar message could come if the mother is leaving. I must emphasize, however, that the feelings parents will inevitably have about these words will be communicated; children tend to have x-ray eyes about their parents' feelings. Hopefully the child can pick up the fact that his grief is genuinely shared, and that all the family members will always be interested in one another's lives and will continue to care for one another. This message too must be repeated, reiterated, communicated in many ways and at many times. An ongoing steadfastness is required in parents, the patience to explain a message over and over again, always accompanied with assurance of love and care from both parents.

The younger the child, the less visible will be the impact of the first messages. And now comes the most controversial aspect of what I have to say, for, despite my strong feelings about the importance of the *family* for the young child, it seems to me that once there is an irreconcilable decision to dissolve such a family, parents should plan, and explain, a clean break from one another. In other words, I feel that the young child would, in most cases, be better off without the usual weekly visits with the parent who has left. He cannot really understand why the parent has left. He will most certainly react to the inevitable emotions engendered by the visits, through one or both parents. There will be recurring confusions, which cannot help stabilize the world of the child.

I realize that there are exceptions. I recently talked to a divorced father of three who said he continued to drive his three children to school each morning. He thus served a useful function for both children and former wife. The children went to different schools, so that intervals between school openings he had daily opportunities to be and to talk with each child. The same father also involved his children in the setting up of his new house on week-ends—shopping, painting, carpentry. The children thus dealt with a reality where they were needed and included; they had contact with their father on a regular basis alone and as a group, in ways that somewhat approximated their former family life. The youngest child sometimes asked him to come and sleep, or come to eat, at "Mommy's" house. His explanation was sufficient for her; he said, "No, I live here now. We are not married anymore. We are divorced, so she lives in the other house, and I live here."

It seems to me, however, that such an arrangement is unusual in maintaining a family group. It is also unusual for the father to offer useful, realistic services, and receive them from the children. Even so, the young child of four still did not quite understand why he did not eat or sleep at Mommy's house. The fact that she seemed satisfied with his explanation is no assurance she really was. Young children are notoriously poor reporters about their thoughts and feelings and experiences. It does not seem helpful to me to subject the child continuously to a perplexity he cannot understand.

Over and again, it seems to me, the visiting between very young child and parent is for the sake of the parent, not for the advantage of the child. There is often a great artificiality in contacts between the child and the parent who has left home. The new home is not set up for young children. Friends, toys, furniture are unfamiliar and unsuitable. Often the parent uses the visiting day for a trip to the zoo, to a park, or museum. A child not fully incorporated into the parents' new life can become an intrusion that makes both parent and child uncomfortable. Also, in most cases a legal break does not ensure immediately harmonious feelings of good will toward the absent spouse. The young, sensitive child can more easily pick up such bad feelings than the reasons for the divorce, or he may pick up a feeling of being too much needed and wanted, too much courted for favor by a single parent. Therefore it becomes extremely important if parents plan visiting privileges with children under five years of age, that they carefully scrutinize the reasons for such visits. How will the visits help the child? They must assure themselves that they are useful, informative, encourage a child to express himself, give the child the information that parents are all right and friendly, that the child will be cared for, will *belong*, will be happy in his own right in a new family. The purpose of the visits should not be just to provide entertainment or special favors. They should not be used to assuage a parent's feelings of guilt, or his inevitable feelings of loss.

Young children flourish best in a stable, orderly routine,

in an environment with which they are thoroughly familiar, and which has in many respects been tailored to their special needs. Visits with the absent parent tend to introduce novelty, confusion, repeated exposure to a puzzling separation. I therefore tend to favor not weekly visits, but an arrangement in which the absent parent could take over the care of the child for a longer period of time. He could then adapt his household, his friends, his way of life to that of the child, creating a family where the child might feel at home.

This arrangement would work best for the five-year-old, and would have to be communicated to him in much the same way as the divorce was communicated—directly, honestly, with unemotional words, and with, if possible, an opportunity first to visit briefly the parent's new home. The message could be, "I have been writing you about my new house, and now I want you to come to live here. Your mother will help you get all your clothes ready, and I will have everything ready for you here." Household members and possible activities should be described and discussed in advance, also how long the child will stay, and when he will be returning to his usual home.

Visiting times together should be planned for the sake of the *child*. The child needs a family, and since his family has broken, he needs very much to belong to a new family. "Family" means parents and children. If a natural parent is absent, a grandfather, grandmother, or other relatives, or friends, or a new husband or wife can gradually move in to create the new unit. The new family, whatever its composition, cannot be the same as the first one, but the resilient child has a better opportunity to belong to a new family when the absent parent releases his family place and allows others to take over. When visiting privileges interfere with a child's adjustment to a new family, they can be harmful.

Bear in mind that my point of view refers to young children
under five, and would not necessarily apply to older children.

Parents contemplating a divorce rarely think through the
complexities of the situation with regard to the children.
External features often occupy their attention: money, job,
friends, property, later living arrangements. The emotional
effect of divorce upon a young child, the fact that the world
of the small child so completely consists of his immediate
family and the importance of parents in his development,
does not enter into initial considerations. Therefore it seems
to me more necessary than at any other time that parents
who have young children and are considering a divorce explain first to *themselves* what a divorce will mean in all its
aspects. In thus explaining divorce they will do well to think
about what there is in a *family* that contributes to a child's
psychological development. There are obviously many
different personal frames of reference. In general, however,
we can assume that the nuclear family, consisting of parents
and children, is the common one in our culture, and that
there are basic contributions from such a family to its members. A human child is long in a state of *dependency*, highly
vulnerable to family influences.

Family living is an experience charged with profound
emotions, not only when the family is together, but when it
is separated. The love parents offer their children depends
somewhat on all the relationships in the family and comes
through all the senses. General tension is also a global factor, easily communicated among family members. Basic issues in psychosocial development have solution or disturbance in early childhood as a child interacts with his parents.[4]
A sense of security and trust in the world is related to infant
experiences. A child must feel he is loved and cared for

physically, that he is fed when hungry, comforted and cuddled when forlorn, protected when physically in danger.

He needs also to establish a self-respecting sense of autonomy. In toddler days he must be permitted to make decisions, important but not physically dangerous. He must not develop feelings of guilt or shame or inadequacy as he tries his wings in independent decision-making. Parents need to respect him and support him in these important first steps. The development of his conscience, his superego, is intimately related to what his parents interpret as right and wrong, and how they have promoted feelings of trust and autonomy.

There is considerable controversy among researchers about the universality and meaning of the Oedipal experience and about the process and importance of a child's *identification* with parent figures. But parents should review current literature on these subjects, not with a view to coming out with clearcut orthodoxies, but in order to sense, as I believe to be true, that: (1) both parents contribute to a young child's psychosocial and sexual development, and (2) children tend to identify with one or both parents, and such identification is involved in the learning process.

The Oedipal theory suggests that young children between the ages of three and five, loving the parent of the opposite sex more than the other, unconsciously wish the other parent dead and gone. The child commonly works through such fantasies, finally accepting and loving both parents. But if the parent of the same sex does indeed go away at this time, and especially if the disappearance is accompanied by manifest hostilities and vituperation, the child, with his tendency to unreasonable belief in magic and omnipotence, may feel that he has caused the separation. When he sees one or both parents unhappy because of the divorce, he may harbor feelings of damaging guilt, believing that he caused the event.

The unified family, however, plays a role in the solution of the Oedipal conflict. Father and mother become parents, and the child responds to them as such.

Identification is the process by which one person tries to become like another person in one or more ways. Identification with the parent of the same sex is an important personality development. But a child does not identify with one parent to the exclusion of the other, nor does the process go on in a limited period of time. Mother's role is mostly related to nurturing. She serves as a model, sensitive to feelings, aware of relationships, loving and protective and accepting. The father represents more the reality of the outside world. With a son, the father is more likely to be demanding, insisting on a work orientation to the world. The father rewards his daughter by his appreciative attitude toward her feminity. The father, indeed, is the stronger sex-typer, tending to have more intense feelings about sex-inappropriate roles. Father would not tolerate fingernail polish on his young son, for example, but mother might put it there.[5] Within the family, the bisexual nature of the human race is communicated. The child learns about marriage and formulates his role as he observes the functioning of the two sexes in his family. The young child's first impression of marriage is the one he obtains from observing the day-to-day life of his father and mother.

In other words, to the very young child, a family is very important. Both father and mother have roles to play that can influence basic foundations in living. It is true that we have no definitive evidence that divorce per se is a sufficient antecedent to a seriously troubled young adulthood.[6] The effects of divorce on a child cannot be studied apart from his whole life experience. In some divorce cases, parents seem to be able to reach an amicable settlement and support each other in relationship to their children.

In some societies or subcultures, fatherless families, multiple mothering, or community families seem to operate well. Margaret Mead makes an important point with regard to such different family organizations, saying that family arrangements that are a normal part of the culture work well in preparing children to fit into that culture.[7]

But no one seriously considering the problem of bringing up young children without two parents in our culture can feel that the way will be easy. In my opinion, the importance of father, mother, and family for the young child is such that, if at all possible, even an *inevitable* divorce, like an inevitable hospitalization, should be postponed if the child is under five years of age. Constant fighting, disagreement, disunity, are indeed upsetting. Yet they are no worse than the child's anxiety about loss, guilt about separation, confusion about belonging. And it is very rare indeed for a child not to be put into a position where he is not forced to choose one parent over the other because the divorced parents vie for the child's favor. There seems to be no way, no matter how we try, to make this easy for the child.

Parents who have limited and distorted feelings, and impaired capacity to love one another or their children, probably cannot take on the arduous task of explaining divorce to themselves before they embark on a separation. Those who can pause to reflect deeply about divorce and its meaning to children will probably ponder long. Such ponderings will surely be profitable, as parents consider the magnitude of the problem and the numerous variables involved in individual situations. Hopefully, they will extend their understandings beyond mine to new insights about the young child who may be deprived of his place in a family.

CHAPTER III

Dr. Graham B. Blaine, Jr. has devoted his career to the perplexing problems of young people and their emotional difficulties. He draws on his extensive experience as Chief of Psychiatry, Harvard University Health Services, to discuss the effects of divorce upon youth. His broad range of medical and counseling experience is reflected in his sympathetic understanding of both children and parents as he deals with the crisis of family disorganization. In addition to his psychiatric services to students at Harvard University and Radcliffe College, Dr. Blaine works with adolescents at the Children's Hospital in Boston. He is the author of Youth and the Hazards of Affluence *and* Patience and Fortitude: The Parent's Guide to Adolescence.

THE EFFECT OF DIVORCE UPON THE PERSONALITY DEVELOPMENT OF CHILDREN AND YOUTH

BY *Graham B. Blaine, Jr.*

WHILE DIVORCE is hardly a desirable sequel to marriage, there are times when it appears to be not only expedient but also sensible both for parents and children. The type of marriage which progressively destroys both partners as it proceeds should be terminated promptly. There are times when the trauma inflicted upon children by the continuation of a marriage would be greater than that brought about by a divorce, provided that in the divorce placement of the children is carefully considered and carried out.

Children, particularly those younger than ten, can tolerate more family discord without distress than most adults realize. Arguments and disputes, even heated ones, can be overheard and observed by children dispassionately. They can be objective about such controversies, and even discuss them humorously among themselves. Anger and frustration are emotions with which they are very familiar, and watching such feelings being openly expressed by their elders may even be reassuring.

Threats of separation or divorce are quite another story. One of the most powerful unconscious fears harbored by a child is that he will be deserted and abandoned by one or both parents. To have this frightening fantasy made real by hearing his mother or father talk about leaving may be deeply disturbing. When a couple cannot refrain from threatening one another with divorce openly and making these threats obvious to the children, either directly or by implication, then a separation which will bring some security and consistency into the family pattern should be seriously considered.

A situation even more difficult for young children to withstand without harm is one in which one parent angrily walks out for a temporary period and then returns unexpectedly, only to repeat the performance a few months later. Children can understand parents not getting along perfectly all the time (they have the same problem with each other), but the actual disruption of the family unit is something they are usually unable to tolerate. The constant threat of such an event can be worse than the reality.

Alcoholism and physical violence are also factors which upset and damage children. Loss of control in a physical sense or as a result of intoxication causes fear in the young because of its unpredictability. Arguments can become routine, with a foreseeable beginning, middle, and end, and conclude with no damage done. But children say with genuine fear in their voices after violence, "I didn't know what was going to happen next." In the case of alcoholism, there is an accompanying embarrassment which makes children unwilling to have friends over to play and often causes them to become isolated and withdrawn at a time when companionship is very important.

If it becomes clear, for whatever reason, that divorce is inevitable, then the question of how long to postpone it may arise. It may be possible to keep a marriage functioning until the children are at an age when they will be less unfavorably affected. In general, divorce or separation does not register with much impact from infancy through the age of three. Very young children are not aware of sex differences and do not have a yen for a distinctively masculine person to any significant degree. As long as the child under three stays with its mother, it will probably not be seriously affected emotionally by the absence of a father.

From three to six, however, the child needs both parents more than at any other period. Intimate feelings toward the parent of the opposite sex occur at this stage of development, and these feelings need to be diluted and modified by counteracting feelings about the other parent. It is very difficult for a child to develop normal attitudes toward others later in life if during this three-to-six interval in his growth he does not have both a mother and a father with whom to interact. This is one of the most traumatic periods for a child to lose a parent through death or divorce.

During the next phase, from six to twelve, there is less need for the presence of both parents, and a shift of the adult figures in the child's life is better tolerated. A process of reconciliation with and imitation of the parent of the same sex is beginning, and if a choice must be made about placement with one parent, the presence of the parent of the same sex is preferable.

Adolescents from twelve to eighteen can usually understand the necessity of divorce or separation, and therefore they may not suffer as much as younger children, except when the result is the loss of the parent of the same sex. During adolescence, the most important task to be accomplished is the formation of an independent and individual identity. For this to take place successfully, the presence of a strong and admired person of the same sex in the environment is absolutely essential. This can be a stepfather, stepmother, family retainer who has distinctive characteristics, a tutor, an uncle, or an aunt who is living in the home. If such an identification figure cannot be included in the plans for the placement of a twelve-to-eighteen-year-old, then divorce should be postponed if at all possible.

Once divorce is definitely decided upon, the custody arrangements for the children usually become a major issue. In determining what is best, a good deal depends on whether or not one parent is to remarry immediately. Long-range psychological studies of individuals followed from infancy to middle age have shown that the two factors most crucial to normal personality development are: first, the presence of an adult man and woman in the home for relatively lengthy periods (it is not necessary that they be the actual parents, nor is it essential that they be the same two adults during the entire childhood and adolescent period); second, a place which can be felt as home. This may be one small room or an entire estate, but it should be as permanent as possible and represent to the child a spot where he can always go—a sanctuary where his own private possessions are kept, a refuge which keeps away the rootless, floating feeling that can be so terrifying to a youngster. Nobody feels more lost than the ten-year-old who has no answer to the question, "Where do you live?" Yet, to reply, "Des Moines and Boston," may be even more embarrassing than saying, "Nowhere."

Providing for each child what comes closest to fulfilling

these two requirements should be the primary goal. Boarding school often seems to be the easiest and most appropriate solution, but for children under twelve it rarely turns out to be successful. More individual adult attention is needed at this age than can be provided by the average boarding school. Teachers may seem to be excellent parent surrogates, but the siblings in such a school are too numerous and too needful themselves to allow any one student the depth of human relationship he needs.

I recall one patient who because of a divorce in his family had been sent to boarding school from the age of nine until college. At twenty-five he still perceived his older friends and associates as schoolteachers and housemasters, believing them to be constantly checking up on him and pleased only when they had caught him in some error. Authority had been a distant and exclusively disciplinary force for so long during his important formative years that he could not envision it as constructively critical. This misconception about the amount of hostility in the world around him had led to personality clashes at work and in his marriage. Firm but friendly discipline, coupled with acceptance, must be part of the upbringing of children younger than twelve, and the atmosphere at the ordinary boarding school does not provide it.

The "six-and-six split" (six months with each parent) would seem on the surface to be the fairest arrangement once the parents have separated, but it has many pitfalls. In the first place, it is hard to feel at home in any house which is lived in only half the year. Roots that have to be pulled up so often, rarely sink in and spread out enough to provide any sense of security. Also, all too often children thus divided are used unintentionally as pawns in the complicated power struggle between divorced husband and wife. Each parent may try to outdo the other in currying favor with the children, and, worst of all, one parent may depreciate the other because of bitterness and antagonism held over from the days before the divorce. There are often complications about means and cost of transportation from one establishment to another, as well as bickering about just when is the most convenient time for each parent to have the children. In the end, the child is frequently left with the feeling that he is a victim of vindictiveness and is valued only for his ability to spy on one parent for the other. Finally, there is the financial pressure, for a child may come to feel that he is only a source of funds for mother and a troublesome expense for father.

A student who had been subjected to this kind of divided living came to me for treatment because of deep depression at the time of the Christmas holidays during his sophomore year at prep school. He had always experienced mild feelings of discouragement at vacation time, but this year it was worse. His depression turned out to be linked to the fact that neither parent wanted to have him home for Christmas: his mother was going to her second husband's family, and his father was planning a honeymoon cruise with his third wife. He had to face up to the fact that for many years he had had no one place that he could call home. He had been unconsciously bothered all along, but until this moment of rejection by both sides of his family, he had not realized the depth of his loneliness. Perhaps it was as well that events turned out as they did, for this severe depression led him to seek psychiatric help and eventually to become better reconciled to his situation.

Living under the year-round custody of one parent with flexible visiting privileges with the other would seem to have many advantages over the six-and-six split, but here, too, there are snags which can cause trouble. Principal among these is the danger of forcing too much responsibility on a young child—depriving him of carefree pleasures which should be part of the years from three to twelve. This occurs most often when a child is placed with the parent of the opposite sex, either alone or with younger brothers and sisters. Then a boy may take on the role of man of the house, share in decision making, help discipline the younger children, and later may even serve as mother's escort on social occasions. This not only tends to make him overly serious and earnest, but also ties him emotionally to his mother in a way which may interfere with his forming relationships with girls his own age throughout life. Likewise, a girl living with her father can quickly adopt a wifelike attitude—preparing meals, cleaning the house, and perhaps playing hostess when friends come in. This can age her before her time and cause her to become uninterested in the activities and dating customs of her contemporaries.

Tragic results can be caused by this kind of placement, as was true in the case of a former patient of mine, a high school senior who committed suicide after running away from his mother's home to his father's place in the South. This boy's parents were divorced when he was fifteen, and against his wishes arrangements were made for him to live with his mother and three younger sisters. He took his responsibilities toward them very seriously, but his schoolwork and his dating relationships did not go well. Several short stays with his father only strengthened this boy's feelings of admiration and respect for him, and the separation became even more intolerable. When a last desperate plea to his father for a chance to live with him was turned down, he decided that life was not worthwhile. Children over twelve must have individuals of their own sex whom they admire close to them in order to identify with them, take advantage of their advice, and follow their example.

Generally speaking, isolating a child from his brothers

and sisters works out badly. Children like to discuss their concerns with each other. They need the reassurance which comes from finding that another shares their feelings and they are not alone in experiencing confusion, loneliness, and resentment over what has happened. No real harm comes from sending siblings in groups of two or more to separate homes, although care should be taken to keep together twins or children close in age or feeling for each other.

As a rule it is not a good idea to let children choose the parent with whom they will live. Often they are afraid of offending one parent; or they may be afraid of punishment if they do not say what they think a harsh parent wants to hear. A child's choice made out of fear is less likely to be the right one than one made by parents or advisers out of their wisdom and experience. In most situations it is best to have the placement of the children firmly decided upon before they are told about the divorce. An interim of uncertainty during which parents, lawyers, and grandparents bicker over what is best for the children makes them feel unwanted and afraid of being abandoned. This can lead to serious guilt and depression.

When a child becomes an adult, he sees the people around him through the same eyes as he saw his parents. His view of men and women will always be influenced by what he saw in his father and mother or those who were substitutes as he grew up. If these significant adults were inconsistent, untrustworthy, unreliable, and deceitful, he will always suspect that these same characteristics lie hidden in all men and women, whether or not there is outward evidence of this in their day-to-day behavior.

Because children's views of their parents are so vitally important in their future orientation to the world at large, the single most important mistake to avoid in situations involving divorce is the depreciation by one parent of the other in the presence of children. If this undermining course is avoided and the other principles outlined above are followed, particularly the making of a home and the presence in it of a healthy adult of the same sex, then the chances of normal development taking place are good, despite the separation of the parents. The children of such a carefully and unselfishly planned divorce can expect to achieve satisfying relationships with their peers and to avoid repeating their parents' mistakes when they face difficulties in their own marriages later in life.

SUMMARY

Divorce in America has become increasingly frequent. Parents approaching or going through it should understand as promptly as they can the ways in which the breaking up of a home affects their offspring. Children, no matter how much they may feign indifference and lack of concern regarding their parents' separation, cannot ever emerge from divorce completely unscathed. On the basis of research and experience, certain definite principles can be laid down which will keep children from being victimized. These can be summarized as follows:

1. Place children with whichever parent remarries unless there is a marked incompatibility between that parent and the children.
2. Children under twelve should not be sent to boarding school.
3. If children must be shuttled between families, then one household should be established as home and the other as a place to visit.
4. Do not give children under twelve a choice regarding the parent with whom they are to live, and do not tell chil-

dren about an impending divorce until definite plans for the future have been agreed upon.

5. Children should not be placed in a position where they serve as confidants or spies for one parent against the other. Every effort should be made to help them retain whatever feelings of love or respect they may have for each parent.

CHAPTER IV

Divorce and the Child: "The Father Question Hour" is a penetrating case history, poignantly illustrating the real day-to-day problems that faced a young boy, his mother, and eventually a stepfather. The mother "became aware of the importance of keeping a record of the questions Jeff was asking her. In the course of recording the dialogues with her son, she revealed how he was trying to work out his need for a father. At the same time, the dialogues showed on her part a wise and courageous confrontation to his questions which inevitably made for an increasingly meaningful relationship for both."

Dr. Stanley H. Cath, is Assistant Clinical Professor, Tufts University School of Medicine, and Member, Boston Psychoanalytic Society and Institute. He recently co-edited Geriatric Psychiatry: Grief, Loss, and Emotional Disorders in the Aging Process.

DIVORCE AND THE CHILD: "THE FATHER QUESTION HOUR"

BY *Stanley H. Cath*

LIFE, OF NECESSITY, includes many unavoidable disappointments, losses, compromises, and renunciations. The Greeks conceptualized this inevitability as *anangké* (ανανηκγ): "what must be" or "inexorable force," a fate to which even the gods must submit. They repeatedly attempted in literature and philosophy to cope with its impact upon the human adult. For a child, one of life's greatest tragedies is the reality loss of a parent. Such loss brings pain that is often felt throughout a lifetime and poses one of the greatest challenges to the child's further development.

It is obvious that the consequences of parental loss will differ according to the many variables of each individual case. How a child responds will be determined by his age at the time of loss, his sex, the presence or non-presence of brothers and sisters, the sex of the lost parent, and the sex of the remaining parent, to suggest but a few of the possible variables. What brought about the loss will also be significant, for each of the situations that bring loss—death, separation, desertion, and divorce—can have its own characteristic attendant psychic and emotional effects upon the individual child.

One cause of loss is, of course, death. But in the world of today, the increase in the number of divorces is fast accounting for many of the parental loss tragedies. Why the divorce rate is increasing is a question far too complex and detailed for this chapter. However, it is sadly obvious that as our population increases and the capacity for our society to develop individuals capable of sustaining marriage increases, so, in proportion, the number of those incapable also increases.

The failure of a marriage is felt with particular poignancy by the child. Marriage is a complicated relationship, involving two people who bring both assets and liabilities to their union. While two people and their children create the family, as individuals each undergoes a restless, continuing struggle for personal integrity as well as collective security. Conflicts that both challenge and define security occur constantly. Even in a state of relative harmony, there are fluctuations between feelings of trust and mistrust, of being in control or being controlled by others, of submission and competition, of activity and passivity, of the need to accrue and the need to share. And all these have something to do with a sense of belonging, of self-respect, and of an emerging capacity to love and be loved. The family is the setting in which these issues are tested over and over again. The intact family, which the young child comes to feel as an extension of the self, gives the child an important self-image that is correspondingly intact.

Accordingly, the breakup of the family unit, for whatever reason, though it creates special problems for each individual member, poses certain particularly difficult problems for the children. The story of Jeff as given in "The Father Question Hour" illustrates in vivid and concrete terms some of the problems facing both mother and child. It shows how it is not just the external events that determine the outcome of loss in terms of eventual ego strength or weakness, but, more often, how these actual events are handled by the victim of the loss, and how this loss is interpreted by significant others around. It is usually no one single event, no one set of attitudes, but rather the day-to-day adjustment in family interaction, and the continual conscious and unconscious interpretation of how the loss has been experienced, that finally brings some understanding of the puzzling question, "Why did it happen to me (or to us)?"—the ultimate question, and one that hints at a frightening undermining of self-esteem; indeed, such day-by-day handling of the problems created by loss may provide eventually for a resolution of that haunting question in retrospect. This universal question can be answered, at best, only qualifiedly and only with some degree of acceptance by those whose ego strength has grown. The loss of a parent may bring a temporary regression or a more permanent ego impairment; in rare cases, it may, happily, prove to be an impetus toward achievement and creative effort, for in the resolution of grief the child may forge new strengths as he tries to repair his wound in order to maintain his faith in the growing of his ego and his surrounding world.

"The Father Question Hour"

The story of Jeff and his mother, it must be noted at the start, is a very unusual one. It might never have assumed its particular interest had not two preconditions existed: an intelligent, sensitive mother, alert to her young son's needs and courageous enough to acknowledge them; and a very intelligent child, seemingly determined to undo his fatherlessness in order to achieve an intact family. The mother, who was in therapy during some of these years, became aware of the importance of keeping a record of the questions Jeff was asking her. In the course of recording the dialogues with her son, she revealed how he was trying to work out his need for a father. At the same time, the dialogues showed on her part a wise and courageous confrontation to his questions which inevitably made for an increasingly meaningful relationship for both. Jeff was a most unusually verbal child. His way of coping was one of several he might have adopted: other children might have acted out their search in other ways—by approaching strange men as they searched for father; by increased aggressiveness as a search for punishment to allay their guilt feelings about parental loss; by the formation of psychosomatic symptoms; or by engaging in a restless search for substitutes via sexuality.

Although the separation of his parents was not culminated until he was a year old, Jeff rarely saw his father after the first six months of his life. The only visible sign he gave of remembering that someone else had lived in his home came when he was nine months old; toward evening if he heard the outer door of the apartment house open, he would turn toward the door as if expecting someone to enter. This sign that he was "missing someone" was apparent for only a few weeks. Subsequently, there were two or three visits from his father, but they ceased shortly before his second birth-day.

When he was about two years of age, he seemed to be-come especially aware of men. It was at this time that he be-came markedly attached to his only uncle, and to Peter, an apartment house neighbor. Both men had a child about Jeff's age. His mother noticed that when he was with these children they seemed openly more possessive of their fathers and talked constantly about their "daddies." Jeff's failure to participate in this kind of conversation indicated to his mother his bewilderment, which she interpreted as his aware-ness of loss, or at least of "not having something." She shared his pain when in his presence her friends took care not to use the word "daddy" when speaking with their chil-dren. Sometimes if the word slipped out, she was conscious of the long silences or the side glances that indicated self-conscious embarrassment so often felt in the presence of a fatherless child. In spite of her own pain during these early years after her divorce, Jeff's mother could realize the degree of her small son's unhappiness. The lump in her throat was for both of them, a lump that decreased in size as time wore on but never entirely disappeared as the desensitization process took place in mother and child. Her ever-present willingness to recognize Jeff's unhappiness is remarkable evidence of her own refusal to give in to self-pity and was, clearly, an important factor in the continuing interaction between her-self and her son.

Thus it was apparent to her long before Jeff could verbal-ize the concept of "fatherlessness" that he realized other chil-dren had something he lacked. As soon as he was able to talk (around two years of age), she learned that his sense of difference had indeed been translated into feelings of depri-vation and loss. This awareness coincided with other dis-coveries a child of that age makes, as he "gets into things" and becomes conscious of the self as a "body" in space that affects things and is affected by them. Families are realized to be extensions of self into the external world. Feelings of power and control, admixed with dependent helplessness, are linked to the extended objects around him.

Jeff did what most children do when afraid to talk about their feelings: he introduced the subject that was closest to his heart by using safer substitutes or displaced objects. One night while preparing for bed, he heard the child of Peter, the upstairs neighbor, crying. "Is Jane crying for her daddy?" he asked. "It sounds that way," his mother replied. "Is Jane's daddy home?" was his next question, betraying that his real concern was with "daddy" and "being home." The many questions about Jane's daddy that followed, questions to which he already knew the answers, revealed to his mother that this was his way of wanting some answers for himself. She finally put an important question to him: "Is there something you would like to ask me?" Thus began what came to be called "the father question hour," a time of questions and answers, of open and honest dialogue between mother and child that usually took place at bedtime, though not restricted to just one time of day.

Jeff's response was immediate, and as courageous as his mother's had been. "Yes," he replied, "where is my daddy? Why doesn't he stay here the way other daddies do?"

Sensitive to his need to understand his difference from other children, his mother chose wisely to answer him as clearly and as simply as she could, regardless of her own unhappiness.

"Because we are divorced, and he lives somewhere else."
"What is divorced mean?"
"Sometimes when two people get married they find out that they didn't love each other, and would be happier living

apart or being married to someone else. The divorce was between your father and myself, and you had nothing to do
with it. Your father wants you to be very happy just as
I do."

"Does he live far away from here?"

"Not very far away; but he lives away from here."

"Where?"

"In an apartment." (Jeff's mother did not feel it necessary
to tell him his father lived only a short walk away.)

"Will he come to see us?"

"No. We both thought that since we would be happier
living apart, it would be better to start again. That is why I
date; so we can find a man we will love, and who will love
us. You can kind of pick your own daddy—won't that be
fun?"

"Did Karen (his cousin) and Janie (Peter's child) pick out
their daddies?"

"No, but your other friend, Louise, can pick out her
daddy because her parents are divorced too."

In his struggle to grasp the concept of "divorce," it was
good for Jeff to know of another child in a similar situation.
Again and again he sought to understand "separation," "not
living with us," and in his bedtime questioning indicated a
regressive clinging and a need for mastery of his mother (and
of his situation) that, nevertheless, came to be beneficial for
both mother and child. Her willingness to listen, to rephrase,
to discuss patiently over and over again the half-true story
that caused her so much pain reveals her remarkable awareness of how very important it was for her small son that
"someone" of great significance had disappeared from his
life. It took a lot of stamina to assure him that his father
"wanted him to be happy" and to reassure him that the
family had broken up through no fault of his. Although one
might question the wisdom of promising him that he "might

pick his own daddy," it was a promise that truly made him different in a "superior" way from his small friends, and it seemed to bring him important support. The fact that the promise later "came true" tended to augment Jeff's sense of omnipotence. At least, it gave him an answer for his friends: "I am looking for a daddy, and I can pick my own."

Children of Jeff's age can be most concrete. Everyone must live somewhere, and since trains are for going away and daddy was away, Jeff understandably concluded, "My father lives on the train tracks." That he was trying to place his father in space as he tried to comprehend the concept of "living or not living" with mother is seen in the following:

> "How come I'm living with just you?"
> "Because your father and I are divorced."
> "Why didn't I live with him?"
> "Aren't you happy living with me?" (Then [wrote his mother], pulling my emotions together for the time being, I added to that overly sensitive, guilt-ridden question of mine): "Also, Jeff, your father works all day and mothers usually take care of the children."
> "I want to live with you, all of us together, I mean."

Jeff's immediate sensitivity to the hurt he had given his mother did not go unnoticed.

> I would venture to say [she commented], that this conversation was not exactly my finest hour! Inside, I was screaming (to myself)—what a joke—live with a father who gave you up, one who didn't even want to visit with you, not to mention ever calling to ask about you. Here I was, left alone with the child, to explain why he can't see his father; left to make the excuses. I knew I wouldn't hurt Jeff that badly to tell him that his father just couldn't care. And yet, I couldn't be a martyr, and take all the blame my son would most under-

standably place on me. As my psychiatrist pointed out, Jeff
would now have to live and relate only to me. I had to learn
that nothing I could say would be the "right" thing, because
Jeff was not in a "right," or "normal" situation. But I could
say a "wrong" thing! Somehow, I had to find a middle
ground where I could be honest with Jeff, without deliberately hurting him or his opinion of himself. I would try to
have us live together with as little resentment as possible.

Children of Jeff's age can abandon painful reality as easily
as they can sometimes be most concretely aware of it. In his
attempt to cope with the fact of fatherlessness, Jeff revealed
his need to secure for himself a "family." He and his friend
Louise began at times to call each other brother and sister.
He called other men "daddy." Ego-boundaries can be fused
and separate identities easily interwoven. His maternal
grandfather had recently died. In the small boy's mind, his
mother's father and his own father were one and the same,
and the death of one explained the absence of the other.

> "Who is that man in the picture?"
> "Your grandpa, Jeff, and my father."
> "Where is he? Why did he go away?"
> "He died because he was very sick, and he's with God
> now. You have his name because you were named after
> him."
> "He is my father too, because my father is dead."
> "No. This is your grandfather; your father did not die."
> "No. My father is dead too."

Jeff's anger made him very emphatic but his mother did
not flinch from insisting on the truth. "I gave the same answer as the previous one, just a little more definite sounding."

Jeff's concern about his departed father began to be attached to his mother, and his possessiveness became more and more openly manifest. It is quite normal for young children to fear that the mother who is out of sight will not return, yet, I think, the intensity of Jeff's desire that his mother be with him continuously was another indication of his awareness of his loss of father. Around the same two-year-old stage he openly resented his mother's leaving at any time. His distress (lightened for a moment by his unconscious pun and his mother's laughter) was evident in a dialogue that was, in a sense, almost typical during this period.

> "Are you going out tonight?"
> "Yes. I'm going out on a date."
> "I want to be your date and go out too!"
> "You're my son, but we still go places together."
> "Do I shine?"

"This was too much altogether," his mother wrote, "and I laughed as I tried to explain the difference between *sun* and *son.*"

> "You have your friends and mommy needs to go out with her friends too."
> "You shouldn't go out and leave me alone."
> "You're never alone. Mary [the baby sitter] is always here when mommy goes out, and stays until I come home."

It is possible only in literature to see clearly the alternate choices facing a character; in "real life" it is only possible to conjecture, and with caution. But the story of Jeff and his mother tempts one to posit "the possible other choice" she (or even Jeff) might have made. One justification for this is, of course, the mother's conscious awareness that she was making decisions of importance for her and her son's future. Thus, in a way, Jeff's story has moments of suspense. This was just such a moment. "I had to reassure him many times that I would not just 'go away,' " his mother said. "I knew I felt guilty about hurting him by insisting that I also needed a life of my own. But I forced myself to go, knowing that the outcome would be tragic if I didn't."

It is important to interrupt Jeff's story at this point and to suggest just how potentially tragic his mother's "wrong" choice of action might have been. The pain of the divorce was, clearly, still an acute one for Jeff's mother. Separation and loss, whether by death or by divorce, is followed by a period of pondering mourning. We know mourning serves an important function. It brings memories and experiences associated with the departed into consciousness. If these memories are mostly pleasant, a feeling of longing predominates; if they are hostile and unpleasant, a feeling of hurt and guilt. In most cases, both occur together, and constitute healthy grief. Grief, a human asset, permits us to reach, eventually, a relative emotional detachment from the painful feeling of loss and of memories of the past so we may live in the present and direct our energies to new sources of love, approval, and affection.

It is generally assumed, not always correctly however, that a year is needed to detach oneself from old objects and begin new relationships. But the period of mourning, whatever its time span, brings with it special problems for the remaining parent and the child. More often than not, the mother (or the father) is not capable of giving much love to others. Absorbed by the loss, sometimes attributing that loss to personal failure, the remaining parent, occupied with the question "why did this happen to me?" has little energy to love or to empathize with the child. We know from clinical experience, as well as from other sorts of records, that a child's response is to feel a double loss. As he senses the withdrawal of his mother (or his father) into depression or into self-centered bitterness, he may feel a confirmation of his own badness and lack of value or worth. In one child's desperate plea, "But you still have me, mommy!" we hear the whole complex interior "rationale" at work.

There is no single moment when Jeff's mother made the initial "right" choice—yet, even at the risk of repeating, it is certainly important to suggest that her alert sensitivity to his preverbal awareness of his fatherlessness, in spite of her own unhappiness, was one such significant moment. Her firm refusal to let Jeff believe his father dead was another such moment. For the child, as for the primitive, death (or loss) does not come about by chance, or by "natural means." In his unconscious, fears of being abandoned are activated by threats of loss in everyday life. If loss does come about, if his fantasies are realized, then it must be because of guilt-laden wishes or because of some wrongdoing. The haunting and ponderous questions, "Why did this happen to me? Why did my father or my mother go away? What could I have done to prevent it? Did I lack something in giving or in demanding too much?" are universal ones.

Aware of his mother's loss, a child also feels a sense of "something missing." Although it is impossible to know how soon a child is aware of the difference between mother and father, it has been reported that infants as young as six months of age seem to respond differently, quantitatively and qualitatively, to the footsteps or the voices of their parents. Fairly convincing arguments can be presented for "preverbal conceptual mental representations" of both mother and father well within the first year of life. Though before twelve weeks of age a child does not seem to be presented with significant problems when there is a mother substitute, it is unquestionable that after this age the mother becomes increasingly indispensable. Even though the father may be noted in some way, the presence of the mother becomes increasingly more significant and more difficult to interrupt and to replace. Whether such a very young child as Jeff realized the early loss of his father as a specific memory is not known. We do know that after a period of a year a young child will not consciously remember a parent who has been away. Jeff's mother's courageous willingness to let herself be questioned over and over again about his lost father, her unflinching honesty and candor in the face of his persistent need, mark other moments of significant choice. In addition to signifying her own refusal to turn entirely inward, they allowed her small son to develop greater freedom in verbalizing his needs—even invited him to establish this freedom and thus, surely, established greater freedom for both in their relationship. A moment's rejection of Jeff's questioning might well have resulted in many years of damage.

Jeff's mother's deliberate search for new relationships was yet another important choice for both mother and child. There were, of course, discomfiting moments.

> I learned he would manage to be rather rude to my dates, if he was in a certain mood [wrote his mother]. I had tried to make it a big treat for him to meet my new friends, but it obviously wasn't! Some examples: At night, coming home from a date with a man Jeff had met several times during the few months I dated him, I would find my son still awake. He had seemed to particularly like this person (while he always seemed in kind of awe of all the men he met). One night, as I said goodnight to this date at the front door, we heard his voice happily singing out from the other room, "damn, damn," over and over for minutes! I hadn't heard anything like this from Jeff before and I didn't make too much of it right then. I couldn't help laughing but this man was appalled; he told me I should have taken Jeff's behavior much more seriously. Indeed that was the last time I ever saw him.

Again, much that is complex is revealed in this almost comic scene. Children are not like adults in the ways they respond to grief. They do not ordinarily express it by overt depression. Rather, they are more likely to "act out" mourning by devious means—by engaging in a restless search for substitutes via sexuality, by psychosomatic symptoms, or by persistent and "plain" bad behavior. Though Jeff's surprising profaneness is a moment of just such "bad behavior" it is, of course, also, and more important, a sign of other things as well: his sensitivity to the fear of loss of his remaining parent; his demands for the sole possession of his mother, demands more than ordinarily excessive because of his singular situation; even his resentment at the threat of another man replacing his lost father (for occasionally a child may deify and idealize a lost parent to the extent that it becomes impossible for anyone to compare with or to replace the lost ideal).

This Jeff's mother seemed to understand. Such understanding, and a sense of humor, helped her to walk the fine line between becoming a martyr to her son's demands and resenting his possessiveness, though, as she said, "By the time Jeff was three, I began to experience battle fatigue."

A child who insists on the exclusive right to his mother and who wishes to eliminate all competitors is difficult for any adult male to accept. The reaction of a date to a woman with a child is, in many ways, complicated enough. Not only is fatherhood actually an imminent prospect with marriage, but what sort of a mother the woman will be is no longer a matter of speculation. Not only can he see what kind of mother the woman he is thinking of marrying is, but his inevitable identification with the child (especially if the child is a boy) may awaken old hostilities to an alarming degree.

Certainly Jeff made it very difficult for his mother's dates. At first it seemed not to matter whether he liked the man or not. "Get him out of here so we can talk!" was his imperious order in the presence of one date. In spite of his mother's reprimands, he did not hide his jealousy nor his desire to wipe out all competition. "Will I always live with you?" he once asked her. To her reasonable answer that he would do so until he was a man and wanted to live elsewhere, he said with determination: "I always want to live with you; and I don't want you to get married." His mother's candid and clear reply, "I'm not marrying anyone yet, but no matter who it is or when, you will always be with me, and you will have a daddy besides," brought forth the firm assertion: "I don't want one." As his mother recorded: "I said we would have to talk about it the next day as I must get back to Ron, who was waiting for me in the living room. Five minutes or so elapsed. Then Jeff called out: 'Has Ron gone yet?' At that point my date took his leave, slamming the door so that the whole place shook. Again Jeff called out from his room: 'Has Ron gone yet?' 'Yes!' I answered and as Jeff started to hum with happiness I sat down and cried, very hard. I didn't know who to hate first!"

Jeff's mother, wisely determined not to yield to her son's possessiveness, continued to date Ron. Once more it is possible to see a moment of significant choice. In spite of his loud assertion, "I don't want one," Jeff did, indeed, want a daddy. As his mother noted:

At times during the nine months I dated Ron, Jeff admitted wanting a father. Usually, before going to bed he would ask, "Is Ron coming over tonight?" A yes or no answer brought the same simple response from him: "Why?" One particular night, after this ritual reply, he started to say his prayers, which usually were as follows: "God bless mommy, Uncle Don," etc. This particular night he added: "God bless mommy *and daddy* and Uncle Don." I noticed his head was turned as though he was afraid to look at me, and I said he could say anything he wanted. He shook his head yes, and said it from that night on. I cannot say it was an easy thing for me to hear, but it was easy to give him permission to say what he felt, because I knew I had to. I, also, had more control by then than I had had at the time when he questioned me about living with his father. I could almost feel the great need in him just to say "daddy." I did find I was a bit shaky after each "father talk" session with my son. The rest of the night was always a depressed one for me.

We know that a father may be lost to a very young child and, for a while, his place filled fairly satisfactorily by a mother. But we also know that such more or less stable situations are of very short duration. That Jeff was reaching the stage when he needed a male in his life was clear. It was an extremely important stage. A son left at an early age with his mother will begin, inevitably, to rebel against maternal domination in his need to reject mother as the ideal model for male behavior. It is at this time (around three or four years of age) that a boy gives evidence of the significance of his old loss, and begins to reveal the degree of vulnerability he has to the traumatic nature of his altered environment. Jeff's mother, at this time, revealed once more her sensitive and intelligent response to her son's needs, even as she showed her continuing courage and openmindedness.

One day in a drug store Jeff pointed to an older man sitting there and asked: "Is that man a father?" I replied, "I think he is. Why do you want to know?" Jeff's comment, "Because I would like him to be my father," found me with only a weak "oh" as a response because I felt like crying. Then I asked Jeff if he would like to go to the toy store and buy a certain truck he had been asking for. I had felt it was too expensive a toy at the time, but at this particular moment I couldn't think of another thing to do. I suppose the word helpless would best describe my mood at the time, as I thought to myself how desperate he must feel to choose a strange man on a soda fountain stool.

This was indeed a critical time for both mother and child. In his growingly overt search for a father, Jeff was beginning to show he was feeling a deprivation of what may be called "building blocks of character structure." Such "building blocks" are essential for further growth, and by adolescence the effectiveness of the particular reparative maneuvers will become evident. For example, a child who has suffered the loss of a father may find himself called upon to give of himself in complex ways. The loss of a partner may mean the loss of sexual life for the parent who is left. The lack of a general outlet often provokes irritability, jitteriness, or apprehension over one's own fantasies. Some become "gay divorcees," whose depth of despair may be expressed by a search for physical gratification, as if one could make up for quality by quantity. The despair, the depression, the frantic "search," combined with feelings of failure, take up tremendous amounts of psychic energy, leaving children depleted of mother's interest. This does not necessarily happen continuously. It may alternate periodically with an opposite (and apparently contradictory—certainly, a confusing) situation: an excessive dependence upon the child on the part of the parent. In this situation, a child may find himself unconsciously called upon to "give to" his parent what, he senses correctly, is felt as missed or lost or gone. The reversal of roles makes him into a little mother, or a motherly father, in order to alleviate the sensed despair of the parent and to allay his own fears of further abandonment. He may attempt to meet his parent's needs by offering to sleep in the place of the missing one.

Some mothers, in their bitterness and pride, claim they have been both mother and father to their children (a claim Jeff's mother resisted the temptation to utter), revealing the storehouse of hostility and resentment retained against the departed partner who is supposedly responsible for the state of affairs. Many times a child may inadvertently reopen the wound by gestures, mannerisms, or other resemblances to the now hated partner. Sometimes this hostility is so great as to lead to false reconstructions of the events leading to the divorce or to the constant devaluation of the departed part-ner. A woman may try continually to prove she was the "better parent." For very deep psychological reasons, she may set up repetitive situations in which she tries to play the role of the father, thereby proving both her and her off-spring's independence of him.

Mother's very real despair may create for the child a be-wildering awareness of her unconscious hostility to him as another male figure, and lead him to abandon the identifica-tion with a male figure who would "do such a thing as im-pregnate a woman and then desert her." Mother may often remind her child that, in contrast to his father, she is "stick-ing by him," thereby adding to the burden of guilt he may feel from having his Oedipal fantasies actualized. For one's magical fantasies of patricide and incest with mother should not be realized. This Oedipal conflict is difficult to resolve under the best conditions, but if the father has actually disappeared from the family scene (whether in death or di-vorce), a child may feel that he has, in his magical omnipo-tence, brought about the disappearance. The consequent feelings of guilt can place tremendous inhibition on the ex-pression of sexual or aggressive strivings later in his life. It is too often that boys raised in such atmospheres are "mother's sons" who come to have problems centering on masculinity, potency, and the capacity to love women. The image of the

mother as seductress or vampire seems almost in proportion
to the child's fear of his own sexuality. The latter can be
neutralized or modified by a father whose presence bears
witness to having survived the Oedipal struggle. The early
disappearance of the father may become rationally explic-
able years later and in retrospect, but it is always felt in
terms of the Oedipal struggle. If one has only fantasies to
supply the answer to the why of the parental disappearance,
they may supply quite a frightening answer indeed. We have
seen how Jeff's mother openly and frankly explained his
father's non-presence as she defined for him, over and over
again, the word "divorce." That Jeff continued to grapple
with the concept for a long time (he was now about three
and a half years old) is clear from the following conversation:

> "Why doesn't my father live here the way other fathers
> do?"
> "Because we are divorced."
> "You both got married, didn't you?"
> "Yes. But once in a while two people find they live hap-
> pier apart, so they get divorced and then they are no longer
> married."
> "You call him up and tell him he's married and he should
> live here with us!"
> "We're not married anymore, Jeff; and I think your father
> is planning to marry someone else now. Someday I will
> marry again, too, and then that man will be your daddy."

Jeff refused to accept his mother's attempt to make way for
a brighter future:

> "You call him up and tell him I said he is married and to
> move in here now!"
> "I'm sorry, Jeff, but I cannot do that. Your father is

marrying again because he wants to. This is his choice, as it will be my choice when I marry again, as it was his choice as well as mine to get a divorce. I know this is hard for you to understand now but this was your father's choice too."

"Well then, marry someone now!"

And he began to list his choices starting with his uncle and then including everyone of his mother's friends' husbands.

"Those men are already married. But we'll find someone who is not married, like Ron—even though it does not have to be Ron—but someone who, like him, is unattached."

"I guess so, if it has to be him."

"It does not *have* to be anyone, and we will meet more men before making up my, and our, mind as to who will be the best husband and father; and someone who we will love, too."

Jeff's mother concluded, later, "My own guilt about his fatherless situation made me convey the feeling that he could choose the man as much as I. Thinking about it now, I believe I overdid it. This was another example of my trying to 'make up' to him."

Jeff's demand that his father return to him even though he had only a short time before (in the fusion of him with his mother's father) believed him dead does not necessarily indicate he understood the concept "divorce" in spite of his mother's patiently reiterated explanation. Such a demand is, for a child, not contradictory. The belief that father is dead is, for many reasons, more reassuring an explanation for deprivation than that father has chosen to go away. The nature of death, i.e., its irreversibility, is almost impossible for small children (if not for most adults) to understand and to accept. Some children who long for the return of the father at the same time live in dread of this return. They suffer greatly in their attempts to keep father's ghost appeased: one may never speak evil of him since his soul is always watching, judging, and waiting for vengeance.

During the next two years, Jeff revealed the ways in which he was attempting to come to terms with his fatherlessness and with his mother's refusal to yield in any important way to his demand for total domination, for exclusive possession, and for a complete elimination of all rivals. Struggling against his growingly explicit need for a male in the family, he continued, nevertheless, to be clear in insisting he wanted no new father. It seemed to him that if she could go out and leave him for other men she deserved to be punished. By almost inevitable logic, he arrived at the conclusion that her "meanness" had been the cause of his father's going away; an appropriate punishment therefore was in his power: "I'll run away from home too!" Jeff's conclusion that his much loved mother was guilty of driving his father away by her "meanness" was neither inconsistent nor surprising. A small child who has only begun to learn to curb his impulses, to accept restrictions, to differentiate cruelty and kindness, feels the incomplete conscience he possesses is the same as that possessed by others, child or adult. Like himself, then, mother can be destructive or loving. The incompleted superego explains why concepts of destruction and murder do not seem to upset a small child to the degree parents often expect. The tolerance of children for violence and for sadism in stories or on T.V. seems sometimes quite remarkable.

A new phase in Jeff's search was triggered when he noticed upon staying overnight with Peter and Sue (the upstairs neighbors), that they shared the same bed. Surprised and puzzled he sought out his mother for questioning. "I explained married people share the same bed, or bedroom." To Jeff this was a tantalizing idea.

Now when he wakened during the night, he would sometimes walk into my room saying: "I want to sleep with you because I feel sick." Or he would say: "Let me sleep in your room because I'm lonely." I always felt sorry for him when he said he was lonely, but I knew I had to be firm about this. I would then tell him he had a lovely room of his own, and there was no reason to sleep in mommy's room. After a while, I just insisted strongly that he "march back into his room immediately." Once when he had a very high fever and I had been up almost all the night I let him sleep in the other bed in my room (out of sheer exhaustion). I realize now that had I been married I never would have done this; however, had I been married there would have been someone else to share the responsibility. I was somewhat frightened whenever he was that sick, wondering if I could handle the emergency. I felt most like an overburdened mother at those times. I knew that my family, or my friends, would be there if really needed, but I had made a personal project of being independent. I thought I had to show the world I could do this alone. Now I realize I had to show myself—perhaps to make up for feelings of insecurity and of failure as a woman, or of being a divorcee and all that implied. I had these neurotic feelings long before I became a divorcee, but being divorced was for me kind of living proof of failure.

Jeff's mother was once more facing squarely a difficult and delicate moment. Any yielding to Jeff's demands for a new kind of intimacy would have been fraught with potential disasters. With his awareness of parental emotions and needs, a child intermittently desires to please and caress, and to provoke and destroy. He may feel limitless in power, but his omnipotence brings terrifying problems which generally precede or highlight the Oedipal stage. If the child learns he can control either his parents or his anxieties by one or another means, he is prone to overdevelop that part of his personality. Jeff's mother's insistence that he be prohibited from adopting the role of "the man of the family" was, if not a "life-saving" decision, certainly a "psychic-saving" one.

Jeff's unconscious need for a male in the family began to be more and more dominant at this time, and began to show signs of winning out over his desire to have his mother all to himself. In other words, his very real need for one of those "building blocks" spoken of earlier became increasingly explicit. The concept of the complementary duality of masculinity and feminity, the actual experience with the presence of both, is of great importance in the construction of "building blocks" in the making of any man. It is necessary to have models onto which one may project positive images of the self, in order later to introject, or take back into the self, these images of what one wants to be like. This is an essential part of one's personality, a nucleus of the ego-ideal and the superego.

For the fatherless boy, subject to maternal domination, the only male model may be the "family image" of the non-present father. The results of the identification may be tragic. If the boy is expected unreasonably to fulfill the role of "the man in the family," he may assume this role is that of a brute, or a deserter. In any case, the taking on of such a role may lead to an impotent preconscious maturity. His identification with the departed male becomes a negative one, since he is deprived of the opportunity to make a more positive, realistic one.

That Jeff was in a greater hurry to find a father than his mother was to find a husband is clear from the following conversation. To her statement that Ron was no longer coming around, Jeff asked:

"Why?"
"Because we did not love each other or wish to marry."

"Why didn't you want to marry him?" I thought I was hearing things [his mother remarked]. He seemed quite angry—guilty too.[1]

"Because I don't want to marry just anyone. We decided not to see each other anymore. No one else had anything to do with this decision."

"Well, I wanted you to marry him!"

"Why, Jeff, I don't think you really even liked Ron very much, did you?"

"Yes, I did so like him."

"But you didn't really love him."

"Oh yes I did!"

Fatigue and exasperation put an end to the dialogue: "I'm sure we will find someone we both like a lot better." Jeff managed to survive this "disappointment" and seemed a happier little boy for not seeing Ron around. Her recognition that Ron had never really given the child a "fair chance" saved Jeff's mother from feeling resentment. Indeed, as she acknowledged:

I was also thankful to be out of an old familiar situation in which I was involved with a half-man, half-child, non-sexual but comfortable figure. I might have made another sorry mistake. It was sure a relief to be rid of Ron and to have to deal only with my own child again.

The experience was a somewhat sobering one for Jeff, tempering to some degree his sense of power over his mother. He seemed to realize that he couldn't have her all to himself, that she had a right to a life of her own, and that they had to live as separate people. He also seemed to have learned to control his anger—not to express it openly in front of her dates, and even to be polite. But he was still free to say anything to his mother in private about his feelings. His mother was learning too: that she had control of her life and possibly the right to want something better, with more promise of future happiness.

If he was not to be allowed to sleep with his mother, there might be some point in other men being able to! By the time he was four, Jeff was asking men to sleep over at his house. The arrangements he proposed were varied but each one insured him his exclusive possession of his mother. Invariably, the men were married and thus clearly unavailable. The invitation was made doubly safe by his proposal that they could sleep with him in his room, or, better still, his mommy could move in with him and the man of the evening could sleep in his mommy's room—alone. The time was both an amusing and a trying one for his mother. I suggest that among some of the motivations for his "new phase" was the fluctuation of his identification during these months from wondering what it was like to be a woman and to sleep with a man, to what it was like to have a baby—a conjecture that seems validated by subsequent conversations recorded by his mother.

For Jeff was making important connections now between men, bed, babies, and fathers, and was beginning to confront the important question of his own birth. "I want a baby," he demanded of his mother one day. "Perhaps after I'm married," was his mother's reply.

"Was I a baby once?"
"Yes, you know you were. Everyone is, in the beginning."
"Were you married when I was born?"
"Yes."
"Who were you married to?"
"Your father."
"What does a man do about the baby in your stomach? Did that man do that to you?"

"I believe I must have looked as stunned as I felt," wrote his mother. "First to hear him put all of this together; then because I was reminded that he was not my son alone! It was sometimes easy to forget he ever had a father. It was also the first time in close to a year he mentioned his father at all."

Then Jeff made up his mind he had found the man he wanted for a father, and, as his mother remarked, the man was, "surprisingly enough, available!" Jeff had "selected" for this important role Murray, a man who, interestingly enough, was clearly attracted to his mother in no small degree because of her remarkable relationship with her small son. He was the son of a very aggressive and domineering woman, and he was fascinated by the unusually close, permissive, but reasonably controlled relationship between the small boy and his young mother. It was as if he could relive, through Jeff, the kind of relationship he might have wished for himself. He was truly kind to the boy, and from the first was a positive influence. Jeff made clear in every way that he could contrive that he wished Murray was his father, his impatience with his mother's cautious deliberation finally leading him to exclaim in exasperation: "Why can't *we* get married now?"

When his mother finally became engaged to Murray, Jeff wanted to know, "What does being engaged mean?" And his response to her explanation was, "You don't need it—just get married!" As his mother commented:

How right he was! We had a very tumultuous engagement, full of indecision and "growing pains," which I am sure had some effect on Jeff. During some of our more difficult periods, Jeff would get concerned about seeing Murray again and ask, "What happens if Murray doesn't become my daddy?" or, "Will I still see Murray and will he still come to see me?" I answered, rather weakly, that he could ask Murray if he wanted to, for I just wanted to end this kind of conversation. Being so unsure of the future myself, I was sure the child would be ruined yet!

But when Jeff learned that his mother and Murray were really going to fulfill his own impatient wish for their marriage, he was silent. In his ambivalence he refused to go to the wedding. Once more his mother revealed her intelligent awareness of the importance of the moment. Knowing that reality, however painful, is always easier to bear than fantasy, she insisted that he be there, for only by being present could he realize that his mother was, in fact, to be married.

"I don't want to go to the wedding."

"Why, all this time you have been telling us how we're all getting married."

"I don't have to go—I saw a wedding on television and I know what it is like now."

"We want you to be with us very much, and we hope you'll change your mind."

Jeff's mother felt very upset about his apparent change of attitude and, for a while, felt hesitant about her course of action. "However, I approached my son again and told him I was buying him a new suit for the wedding."

"I'm not going."

"Yes, you are going because we will all be upset if you're not there. You won't have to do anything but stand there and watch. Afterwards your grandmother is taking us out for a lovely dinner party."

"I really don't have to do anything?"

"Just have a nice time."

"Can my friends come?"

"No, because you're a special guest, because it is your

mommy's and daddy's wedding. You'll be the only child who can come—isn't that exciting? Not many children get to see their mommy get married and go to a late party."

It was clear that Jeff was impressed. He couldn't wait to tell his friends about the treat he was to have. His mother wrote:

He was not exactly bubbling over with enthusiasm, but he had faced the fact that he was going. He was probably feeling so many contradictory feelings that he needed us to insist upon his being there. Now, I'm so glad he was there, or he would have missed out on one of the important events in his life, and, I feel, would not have adjusted so well, or so fast. He still comes out with remarks like: "Remember when I saw you and daddy get married? I danced that night. I liked everyone." He is also very proud to tell his friends that he was at the wedding. It is no longer foremost in his mind, but when he does mention it, he only speaks of how wonderful it was.

At the wedding Jeff tried to stand between his mother and Murray as if he were the one getting married, or perhaps as if making one final attempt to eliminate the rival male by separating the bridal couple. In truth, the marriage was a new contract for him as well, for after the ceremony he asked, "Are we married already?"

A typical reaction of a child to a mother's remarriage is to deny its reality, particularly in the time of the honeymoon. Jeff did this to some degree, disturbed as he obviously was by the arrival of a new double bed, and by the imminent departure of his mother. He became occupied with his own "honeymoon vacation" that was to be spent with his grandparents and with the anticipation of the hours to be passed at the swimming pool with his cousin Karen. But that he also felt the reality of the marriage was clear in the way he consoled himself during the visit for his mother's absence by bragging of his new daddy.

For a time after the return of the newlyweds, Jeff revealed his need by devoting his "question hour" once more to sleeping arrangements. He became, in effect, a night watchman, listening for signs of activity between his parents, and in the morning could often be found sitting at their bedroom door. But, compared to many similarly reestablished families, the complex process of transition to a new family group took in Jeff's case a relatively short time. The movement from overt concern with the question "what will that man do to mommy" to acceptance of the newcomer as "daddy" was for Jeff a progression from negation through puzzled anxiety to neighborhood announcements of the new family structure, including the descriptions of the new sleeping arrangements. Opening the window that faced the parking lot to say hello to some friends Jeff yelled out with obvious joy and pride: "My mommy is married now, and I have a new daddy, and my mommy has one bed now instead of two, and my mommy and my new daddy sleep in one bed together!" His mother, though recording her own "bright red" embarrassment at the sudden publicity, rejoiced in her small son's acceptance, and evident happiness. It had taken but four weeks for Jeff to learn that the two once disparate concepts —Murray and daddy—were one and the same, his transition once more helped by the patient understanding of two intelligent adults.

Much as a sleeper deprived of dreams for several nights dreams in great quantities, as if to satisfy a basic biological urge, a child deprived of a male pattern on which to model himself, craves such an object. The loss of a father, even though wished for at times, never works out in reality as in fantasy because of the sense of "something missing" in the self. In truth, there is gone from the environment an important means of mastering life's problems. Without a viable paternal instructor, children are prone to orient themselves by peer examples or by the model derived from the female. This augmented dependency results either in great insecurity or in a tremendous need to deny the importance of women and to rebel against them. Thus a fatherless boy may also become increasingly motherless, or may grow into an adult without ideals or models to incorporate. He exercises apparently autonomous functions, but is, in fact, governed by them. He has no chance to temper fantasy with the reality of a relationship that involves give and take, to temper jealousies and masculine aggressiveness by interaction and resolution. Jeff, now freed of his sense of deprivation and at the age when his hunger for a male figure was becoming most critically acute, began to devour his new father, as if to make up for lost time and for lonely years. With remarkable patience the newlyweds handled his need, as he sought to adjust, to readjust, and to redistribute emotional love and attention within the family, demanding the sole attention of his new father with the same intensity he had once demanded his mother's. He was clearly "feeling" his now intact family, adding one more of the important "building blocks" to his character structure.

As time went on, Jeff grew less demanding, less insistently possessive. Murray's continued presence, his being with him "in the flesh," made him a "real daddy" in Jeff's mind. It was not long before it was possible for him to accept his mother's request that he no longer mention his own father in his nightly prayers, a request that once more revealed her rather extraordinary capacity to empathize—this time with Murray.

Jeff's usual bedtime prayer had now become "God bless mommy, daddy, Don, and my new daddy." After a few

weeks, I noticed that Murray was not taking this too well—
so I decided to take a gamble. I interrupted him as he said
"my new daddy," and said: "You already said 'God bless
daddy' once. Why do you repeat it a second time?" I pre-
tended to ignore the words new daddy. Jeff looked somewhat
bewildered, stared at me, then at Murray, started to answer
but clearly did not know what to say. After a few minutes,
looking directly at Murray, Jeff said: "God bless mommy,
daddy, and Uncle Don." It has been that way ever since. A
few days later the following conversation took place:
   "Did Karen (Don's child) pick her daddy too?"
   "No."
   "Is Don her first daddy?"
   "Yes, he is."
   "Does that mean he is her 'real daddy'?"
   "Yes. If he's her daddy, then he's a real daddy. Your
daddy is your daddy now, so he's a real daddy too."
   "Does that mean he's not my first daddy though?"
   "No, he's not your first daddy, but that doesn't mean that
he's not a real daddy to you."

According to his mother, Jeff seemed satisfied.

   I don't know if I said the "right" thing. I know that I was
trying to fix the truth, but I did not hide the fact that Murray was not his first father, nor did I lie to him about anything. I felt that Jeff might be young enough to forget the
time "before you were my daddy," as he so often says to
Murray. He has no memory of any other father; Murray is
the only father he will have, unless the day comes when he
wishes to see his first father. Then that will be his choice, and
a free one. Now, however, Jeff and Murray have a real relationship, and, I believe, much love for each other. Still
Murray is sensitive to any mention of Jeff's first father. He
has legally adopted Jeff and feels he is his son, and that's

it! All things considered, I am not sorry for misunderstanding or misinterpreting Jeff's definition of "real."

In this interchange of question and answer, Jeff and his mother were encountering a problem that is not characteristic just of children in divorced situations. Children from intact, normal homes (having both parents present) are curious and often very anxious about pending or actual divorce in the families of their friends. This is so because they share the common fantasy of potential loss of a parent and, also, the belief in their own magical powers. The adopted child, like the child from a broken home, has an unusual appreciation of the powers of destructiveness at his "command," with certain ego modifications as a result. Jeff's conflicts and anxieties were not greatly unlike those of an adopted child. Indeed, at this critical moment when his mother insisted he recognize Murray as his daddy, he was facing something equivalent to that faced by the adopted child.[2]

Jeff's "father question hour" is likely to continue interruptedly, although in modified form. One needs to be prepared for such investigations, such special questions throughout almost all his life from a child who has lost a parent. And a particular form of guilt may characterize children such as Jeff. This was rather poignantly revealed when Jeff, hearing of the birth of a new cousin and unconsciously aware of the link between babies and hurting, as well as between babies and punishment by spanking, once more asked about his father:

> "Was there a man here when I was born?"
> "Yes."
> "Did he go to work?"

"Yes."

"Who was he?"

"I just looked at Murray," wrote his mother. "What should I say to Jeff in front of Murray?" "His name," Murray took up the question, "was Raymond Pierce." Jeff, knowing that Pierce was his own last name, turned to his mother once more:

> "Did that man spank me when I cried?"
>
> "No. Why would anyone spank you as a baby, if you cried?"
>
> "Did you spank me?"
>
> "Of course not. You were a wonderful, adorable baby, and there was no need to spank you. You were my baby and I loved you very much, as I do now."

Jeff was once more betraying guilty anxiety about his own father's disappearance and linking the birth of his cousin to his birth to his fatherlessness to spanking and punishment, then, the part so difficult to believe, all together to intercourse, babies, and what "was done to mother." For, although Jeff is proud of his new father and still brags about him, he at times still resents him and wishes he had his mother to himself. It is probably because of his wish to eliminate competition and his awareness that it is possible to suffer punishment (spanking) from a man that, currently, the ancient disappearance of his first father is recharged by the aggressive guilt found in the normal parental situation.

However, the tendency to push into the unconscious the earliest years of life (infantile repression) goes on. Jeff, if permitted, will "forget" his first father. This his mother has clearly been aware of. With his new opportunity to resolve a normal triangular relationship between a child and parents, the desired identity of a young man who can relinquish early love objects will be easier to achieve. Jeff now has a father whom he can watch closely to learn how a male deals with emotions like anger and love. There will be little danger that he will deify his own absent father, that he will thus come to idealize men and establish overly high standards for male mental and behavioral life. Such exaggerated valuations heighten the homosexual tendency that exists in every child. As he approaches the latency period (after seven or eight years of age) Jeff no longer faces another consequence of fatherlessness. It is during this period a father provides a model in the arena of play and competition, even though much competition is lived out with other children of the same sex and age. Mothers most often fail their sons at this particular time, for they are afraid of the normal aggressiveness in this age group. To escape female domination a boy finds masculine support as a boy among boys, forming in the usual exaggerated devaluing of women. If the mother meets such devaluation with the masochistic defense, "Look at all I've done for you—now you're turning away and abandoning me like your father did," the boy may resort to even more pronounced aggressiveness. In her attempt "to be all" to the child, the mother may exert control by activating feelings of guilt. The boy, having experienced one loss, is so terrified of another that he may yield and surrender his masculinity, or act out his guilt and fear in other destructive ways. In order to maintain true tenderness toward women while also developing an empathetic relationship with other men, a boy requires an adult male with whom to interact. It is with the working through of this complex triangular relationship that one may achieve sufficiently high degrees of self-esteem, of aggressiveness, and of sexuality for potent and effective relationships in later life. To be potent is premised on an unconscious conclusion, namely, that instinctual forces and products do not impinge upon the rights or existence of another human being. It also means that one is not thereby subject to extremely harsh self-restrictions on aggression, lest others be upset.

Jeff's mother's awareness of his need for a father seems to have been as significant a part of her motivation for an early reentry into the dating process as was her own understandable need for a husband. Her courageous handling of her son helped him overcome his hostility toward a new rival while still maintaining his loving relationship with her. Predictably, the full integration of his stepchildedness, with the mysteries of birth, of maleness and femaleness, with concepts of activity and passivity, with curiosity about and respect for tradition, will not take place until adolescent years, during which time his quest for his real father may be expected to reemerge. One can only hope the solidly meaningful relationship with his stepfather will carry him through this difficult period with a minimum of strain, for it is possible, of course, that this particular child may feel a burden of guilty hostility that may challenge his "belongingness" and "maleness" with somewhat unusual severity.

In the meantime, Jeff is on a more promising path than other children in a similar situation might have been. He has the presence of a loving father and the continuing relationship with a mother whose intelligent understanding seems not to falter. So his mother in her closing words speaks wisely and well:

> There are many times I wonder if Murray knew how much he was getting in for in marrying me. Jeff often resents his new father's disciplining, and comes running to me. Then I see Murray feels badly. On the other hand, there are times I must be jealous because Murray is now Jeff's idol. However, I know that Jeff needed a male figure as much as

any child, and the resentment passes, because I am so much more happy my son has what he wanted and needed. Thinking back over the past five years, I can see how much things have changed—for the better. I think that even for a more normal, well-adjusted person than I was, divorce brings out inevitably a "failure complex." I remember compensating by having Jeff perfectly dressed; or by having the biggest and nicest birthday parties; and wanting to die every time he misbehaved in front of other people. I expected too much from Jeff to bolster my personal image. I gradually realized this behavior accomplished nothing except, perhaps, to make a fairly happy little boy, considering his situation, into a very nervous one. I also began to see that I had identified too much with him. I knew all too well what this could mean (mother's boy). My toughest (conscious) battle was to "let go," to let my brother or a few "father" friends take over when around Jeff. Neither big birthday parties nor the expensive presents compensated for his need of a father. and, most of all, neither could his mother.

While no one can know the future, it seems safe to say that Jeff is on the way to establishing new identifications that will work constructively in the ongoing formation of his personality, that he is accepting the reality of the current situation even as he is learning about his past, that many of his misconceptions have been corrected through the slow working through of loss during the "father question" hours, and that the chances he would link a stepparent (a man) to a wicked parent have been minimized both by his internalized attitudes and by the reality circumstances surrounding his mother's remarriage.

CHAPTER V

The dictionary defines divorce as a "legal dissolution of the marriage relation." In the following chapter, Mr. Freedman explains this "legal dissolution," especially as it pertains to the well-being of the children.

Both the courts and the attorneys are concerned with the division of family property and alimony. However, most important in the course of matrimonial litigation is the custody of the children. What will be best for the offspring and contribute to their future development? The attorney chosen for the divorce proceedings must therefore be concerned more with the welfare of the children than with the extent of victory for his client.

Haskell C. Freedman has served as a lawyer in over two thousand divorce cases. A graduate of Harvard Law School (LL.B.), he is a partner in Brown, Rudnick, Freed, and Gesmer, Counselors at Law. One of his most important concerns is young people. He served for eight years as Chairman of the Newton (Massachusetts) School Committee and is a lecturer at the Boston University School of Education.

THE CHILD AND LEGAL PROCEDURES OF DIVORCE

BY *Haskell C. Freedman*

DIVORCE IS a traumatic experience. It not only affects the adults involved but too often adversely affects the children of the marriage.

It is incumbent upon the father and mother to realize that negative consequences of their difficulties and differences should not be extended to their children.

Parental love, family unity, and emotional security are essential to the healthy development of a child. Divorce divides parental love, destroys the family unity, and threatens the emotional security of a child. The child is owed, at the very least, an explanation. What the child should be told, when, how, and by whom will depend upon the facts in the individual case and in particular the age of the child.

The parents must remember that divorce might well have solved their problems but unless the child's right to know and understand what has taken place is recognized and honored in a manner consistent with the child's emotional stability and age then the child's negative reaction to the divorce will be a continuing problem with far-reaching consequences.

DIVORCE PROCEDURE

Parents cannot explain divorce and its consequences to children unless they have some knowledge of the subject themselves. It is not this writer's intention here to do more than set forth certain basic legal principles and procedures of divorce that are in force in nearly all the states. Then, as the focal point of this book is the children, aspects of the award of custody of children will be discussed.

In earlier times, before America was settled, divorce was entirely a matter of ecclesiastical law and therefore under the jurisdiction of the church. Nowadays however, in all the states, divorce is a matter of statutory procedure, and there is no "common law" of divorce.

All of the states have laws relating to divorce and the specific grounds for which a divorce may be granted. Adultery is the only ground acceptable in all the states. Cruel and abusive treatment, desertion, and intoxication are next in order of frequency. Other grounds range from non-support to incompatibility. Massachusetts, as a sample state, offers seven grounds to the wife, namely, adultery, impotency, desertion for two consecutive years prior to time of suit, gross and confirmed habits of intoxication caused by the voluntary and excessive use of drugs or liquor, cruelty, sentence to confinement for five years or more in a penal institution, and non-support. The first six are available to the husband.

The moving party, one seeking the divorce, is usually called the libellant, petitioner, or complainant. The party against whom the divorce is sought is called the libellee, respondent, or defendant. Here I will use the terms libellant, libellee, and libel.

The proceedings begin by the filing of the libel in court. The libel ordinarily contains the names and addresses of the parties, the date and place of marriage, the names and dates of birth of the children, the ground or grounds on which the divorce is sought, and a request for alimony and custody of and support for minor children.

The assumption is that the parties are living apart, and when the wife is the libellant and there are minor children her attorney will at the time he files the libel in court obtain an *ex parte* order giving her temporary custody of the minor children and sometimes, in addition, when the circumstances indicate, a temporary restraining order forbidding the husband from interfering with her personal liberty. The latter two temporary orders may be granted by the court without notice to the husband and without his presence or his attorney's presence in court.

After the libel is filed in court a citation or order of notice issues from the court, which is required to be served upon the libellee. This notice briefly summarizes the contents of the libel and, in particular, states the period of time by which he is required to appear personally or by an attorney if he intends to contest the libel. If the libellee is alleged to be in the state, then this order of notice must be served personally upon the libellee. After the notice has been personally served upon the libellee, the wife's attorney can then require the husband to appear in court on her motion for temporary alimony and support for the children. If the libellee is not in the state, then the order of notice is usually served by mailing to his last known address, by publication in a local newspaper, and sometimes by personal service at the place where he is living or by a combination of one or more of these methods.

The order of notice thus served upon the libellee advises him of the pending divorce proceedings and of the ground or grounds on which the divorce is sought, whether or not alimony is requested, and whether or not custody of and support for minor children is sought.

At this point, if the libellee does not intend to contest he may do nothing and in due time the libellant's attorney will assign the case for trial and it will proceed uncontested.

If the libellee intends to contest the action, he will have his attorney file an appearance for him in court within the time specified in the order of notice. If the libellee does not object in principle to the libellant being granted a divorce but does want to be heard with respect to any order for alimony and custody of and support for minor children, he will, likewise, cause an appearance to be filed for him indicating a contest. In addition to filing an appearance, a libellee may file a cross libel for divorce or an answer in which he will deny the allegations stated by the wife and also set forth affirmative answers wherein he may allege the libellant guilty of a marital wrong or wrongs (grounds for divorce).

In general, for a divorce to be granted the court must ultimately find that the libellant is innocent of any marital wrong and that the libellee is guilty. This is an archaic rule that is in force in practically all the jurisdictions. If the court, after a contest, should find both wife and husband guilty of marital wrongs, then usually neither party is granted a divorce and they are left in status quo.

After the libel and answer are filed in court, the parties can usually avail themselves of certain discovery proceedings such as taking oral depositions and submission of written interrogatories to the other to be answered under oath in order to obtain additional information to support the position taken.

Only a small percentage of divorce cases result in contested trials despite the ostensible contest indicated when the libellee files an appearance or even an appearance and answer.

Ordinarily, after the libellee has been served, the parties, through their attorneys, negotiate a settlement and the final terms are set forth in a marital agreement. Some of the common provisions of such agreements relate to alimony, custody of and support for children, visitation rights, insurance benefits, disposition of real estate and personal property owned by the parties individually and jointly, college education for the children, and medical, dental, and health needs. The agreement may also provide that in event of a dispute as to the interpretation of the agreement, the issue be decided by arbitration in the manner provided in the agreement.

The execution of such an agreement usually indicates that the divorce action will not be challenged on the merits, and the parties will usually submit the agreement to the court at the time of the trial. The parties may provide in the agreement that it shall be incorporated in and be made a part of the divorce decree. In such a case, any of the provisions in the agreement are subject to later modification by the court on a pleading instituted by either party supported by proof of a material change in circumstances.

On the other hand, the parties may provide in the agreement that although the agreement may be shown to the court (as it must be if the judge requests), nevertheless it is not to be made part of the divorce decree but shall survive as an independent contractual agreement between the parties. In such an event, the wife and husband will be usually contractually bound by the terms of the agreement as they relate to provisions affecting each of them, but nevertheless all provisions relating to the minor children are always open to the court by application for later relief by either party, as the children in all divorce cases are wards of the estate. Any decree granting custody of children, and provisions relating thereto, are always subject to modification by the court, as the state in granting the divorce always retains jurisdiction over the children until they reach majority.

Factors determining award of custody

Under the Common Law of England, in event of a divorce or separation, the father had a natural right to custody of children of the marriage regardless of age or sex. This right was only limited by proof of his unfitness by ill treatment of the child. The mother was not considered to have any right to custody. This arbitrary rule of law has since become substantially modified with the increased recognition of the equal status of women and the passage of humane and enlightened legislation tending to equalize the rights of married women and men. Today when a husband and wife, having children, are living together they jointly have custody of their children.

The difficulty arises when separation or divorce proceedings are instituted by one spouse against the other. In such a case, the submission of the marital dispute to a court of competent jurisdiction gives to the court the power to determine custody of children. In such a case, neither parent, all things being equal, has a paramount right to custody. Both parents stand on equal ground.

The general rule of law applicable to the determination of the custody question is that custody is granted in accordance with what is for the best interests and welfare of the child. An example of the language frequently found in court decisions is the following quotation from a Pennsylvania case; the court said:

> In determining the custody of a child of tender years, there is only polestar, one compass, one standard of reasoning to follow, and that is the best interest of the child.

However, the answer may well be the father and in some cases neither parent but a maternal or paternal relation; and in some cases by placement with a child agency, public or private.

In trying to determine what is for the best interests and welfare of the child (or "welfare and happiness of the child" or "best interests of the child," etc.) the courts must and do consider various factors.

Among the factors that courts consider are age, health, and sex of the child; preference of child if of an age when the child can express a rational and logical choice; character of the disputing parents; economic circumstances of the father and mother; and comparable factors, some precise and some imprecise.

Usually the answer is that the welfare and happiness of the child is best served by an award of custody to the mother.

Courts have awarded custody of minor children to the mother despite proof of the mother's adultery. Custody has been granted to a father when the mother was found to be emotionally unstable. Each case stands alone and the judge must decide what is best for the child.

Visitation rights

The judge hearing the divorce case has the inherent power to determine the visitation rights of the parent who does not have custody. Ordinarily, the mother is given custody and, accordingly, the father's visitation rights must be determined, consistent with the ages and schedules of the children, and also with his job requirements and his free time. The judge will listen to the positions of the parents and after taking into consideration their views, frequently divergent, he will then state the hours of the day and the day or days during the week when the father may visit or have the children visit him, and this decision becomes part of the divorce decree.

Alternatively, the parties may come to an agreement with respect to visitation rights prior to the trial. This agreement will then be submitted to the judge, who will ordinarily accept it and make such agreement part of the divorce decree.

The portion of a divorce decree relating to visitation rights, whether as determined by the judge or as agreed upon by the parties and accepted by the judge, can read in different ways.

If the parties are in accord that the interests of the children are paramount and trust each other to cooperate for the children's welfare, the language of the decree may read ". . . and the father shall have the right to visit and to have the children visit him at all reasonable times and places." This general language assumes that the parents will give and take, and work together to maintain a good relationship between the children and the father.

At the other extreme, either by decision of the judge or by agreement of the parties, the decree may read ". . . and the father shall have the right to visit and to have the children visit him each Wednesday from three to five o'clock

P.M. and Saturdays from ten to five o'clock P.M. and on New Year's Day, Easter Sunday, July 4, and Labor Day, and in addition shall have the right to have the children for a two-week period during the summer vacation." This latter type of decree can and usually does provide for all variations of allocation of holidays, school vacation periods, and other free time of the children.

Where the parties are antagonistic, lawyers spend a disproportionate amount of time seeking a form of agreement on visitation rights that both parties will accept.

The mother seldom will agree to any right to have very young children visit with the father away from the mother's home. In such cases if there are several children, the father will have to make the necessary adjustments in order to visit the young child or children at the mother's home and to take the older child or children away with him.

The ordinary decree concerning visitation rights does spell out the *rights* of the parties, but does not specify inherent *responsibilities* of the parties.

Too frequently the mother or the father will accuse the other of misbehavior with the children. One will often accuse the other of (a) not calling for the children on time or not having the children ready on time, (b) not bringing the children back on time or of bringing them back earlier than was arranged and when no one was home to receive the children, (c) "buying" the children's affections by acceding to requests for extra candy and sweets or by unilaterally buying the children expensive toys, (d) interrogating the children as to the behavior of the other, (e) telling the children matters "in confidence," (f) sending the children to the father dirty and in old clothes, or of returning them to the mother dirty and with clothes torn, (g) extreme permissiveness toward the children in order to encourage affection of the children, and of many other acts designed to injure the relations of the children with the other parent.

Some or all of these recriminatory situations can be avoided in whole or in part if the decree granting custody and visitation rights also refers to the responsibilities of the parents.

In this connection the District Court, Family Division, in Hennepin County, Minnesota, uses a "Supplemental Order for Custody" originated by Judge Lindsay Arthur. The decree provides for an award of custody and times of visitation and then incorporates a supplemental printed order which reads as follows:

These provisions relating to custody, alimony, support, visitation and conduct of the parties, are subject to the following terms and conditions:

A. Care and Supervision—The party who has custody of the children, hereinafter referred to as the Custodian, will provide the children (a) with regular and nutritious food, (b) with clean and appropriate clothing, (c) with sanitary and reasonably private living and sleeping quarters, (d) with appropriate medical examinations and treatments, and (e) with guidance and counsel in worldly and spiritual matters. The Custodian will (f) train the children to obey and respect their teachers and the law, (g) will require the children to attend all regular sessions of school until graduation unless excused for medical reasons or by the school or by the Court, (h) will personally supervise and control the conduct and activities of the children except when they are at school, or in known and usual recreational activities, or in the immediate care of another competent person. The Custodian will not (i) engage in, or permit in the presence of the children, any excessive drinking, immoral conduct, obscenities, violence, or disrespect for law and order. The Custodian will advise persons entitled to visitation of (j) all school or police disciplinary contacts, (k) all medical contacts, and reports, (1) all other important developments in the lives and activities of the children.

B. Control of Visitation—Unless otherwise provided, (a) the person having visitation may take the children to such reasonable places for such reasonable activities as such person may determine, (b) the Custodian will have the children ready and available promptly for all visits, (c) if advised in advance, the Custodian will provide the children with such ´special and additional clothing as may be appropriate for the planned activities, (d) in the event a child is invited or desires to participate in other activities which may interfere with a visit, the Custodian will not encourage, permit, or consent thereto without previous approval of the person whose visitation will be interfered with, and will not deprecate the denial of such approval, (e) the person entitled to visitation may correspond with the children and Custodian shall not censor such correspondence, (f) the person entitled to visitation may telephone each child for (*sic*) not to exceed 15 minutes between 7:00 P.M. and 9:00 P.M. on Wednesdays and Sundays and at such other times as the parties may agree and the Custodian shall not participate in such calls, (g) the Custodian may not reduce or deny visitation for failure of support.

EFFECTS OF DIVORCE ON CHILDREN

Environmental factors governing the upbringing of the child, and primarily the parental relationships prior to the divorce, to a large extent will determine the child's ability to accept a divorce situation without undue stress.

In the first instant, a conflict is presented. When one or both parents want a divorce, the child or children are usually against it. Children ordinarily want to preserve the home and to live with both parents. It might well be said that a stable intact home is a natural right of the child. The law, however, does provide for termination of a marriage, and thus the home and the children are forced without any formal expression of their views to live with the decision. In many cases it may well be argued that a divorce will ultimately be better for the children than continuation of a home where one spouse has wholly failed to honor legal and moral familial obligations. Yet it is true, too often, that a spouse seeks a divorce for whim or caprice or less than valid reasons, and subordinates the interests of the child to personal, selfish reasons.

Divorce has and can occur without any substantial negative effects on the children. Statistics on this point are not easily available but experience does indicate that it happens.

But children are hurt by divorce. The harm suffered by children is manifest in many ways. Frequently the child will develop psychosomatic illness; a mother will often lay undue burdens on a minor son as the new head of the family; either parent, the one with custody or the other, may seek to maintain or purchase the affection of the child by gifts, cash, allowances, and other monetary indulgences; the child can be hurt by recrimination by either parent against the other after the divorce; a young boy too often finds it difficult to grow up without a father in the house; some children feel that a divorce means a rejection by the divorced parent; the emotionally immature or unstable mother too often indulges and spoils the children; the divorced parents more often than not compete for the affection of the children; parents frequently "confide" in minor children too young to accept the parents' problems; and this indictment could go on and on.

The burdens upon children in growing up to be relatively

normal and successful citizens in today's society are sufficiently heavy without the added problems caused by their
parents' divorce.

The important question

Is it better for the children that there be no divorce regardless of the grounds available to a spouse seeking one?

This question must always be answered by the party seeking the divorce.

There is no simple answer. A great deal depends on the
validity of the grounds suggested by the spouse seeking the
divorce, the ages of the children, and whether or not a bona
fide effort has been made or can be made to maintain the
marriage.

The lawyer, when questioning the spouse seeking the divorce, too often will ascertain that the grounds upon which
his client seeks a divorce are not valid in the sense that they
probably could not withstand a contest by the other spouse
and could only prevail if the divorce hearing was to be uncontested, with the implied consent of the other party required. In such a situation, an agreement with the other
spouse is required before moving ahead. The lawyer here
has, in my opinion, the obligation to challenge his client to
consider the effect of the divorce on the children. The living
conditions at home, the chronological and emotional maturity or immaturity of the children, and the economics involved in the maintenance of two living establishments have
to be considered. There are no blanket answers for all cases.
When children are of adult age and the wife has for years
lived with a man who has been an alcoholic, a compulsive
gambler, a personally unclean person, an adulterer, a person
who has physically abused the wife, or has behaved in a
comparably destructive manner, then the answer is not too
difficult. If she also has independent means and will not be

dependent upon alimony from the husband, then the answer is clearly in the affirmative. If the wife will be dependent upon an order for alimony for total support or to supplement her own earning ability, the client will have to weigh the factors involved.

At the other extreme, a young wife with one or more minor children under four years of age tells her lawyer a story of unhappiness involving physical cruelty, adultery, and neglect. Does she seek divorce at this time, when the children are young enough so that the full impact of the loss of the father may not be too apparent, giving the mother a chance to raise the children in a harmonious household? Or does she continue with the marriage with the hope that any father in the house is better than none?

Many times the decision has already been made. The wife knows that the present living conditions are harmfully affecting the children. Bedwetting, nervousness, insecurity, withdrawal, and other negative emotional symptoms may indicate that things will not improve without a separation of the parents.

What to tell the children

The answer to this question depends upon the age and emotional stability of the child. In any event it is doubtful if there is any answer that will satisfy all children.

When the children are quite young, it may be sufficient to simply state that the parents have decided to live apart, that both parents love the child, and that the one moving out certainly will visit and see the child. Simple, brief, and truthful statements are in order.

When the children are old enough to understand the nature of divorce, a somewhat more detailed explanation may be appropriate. Frequently, and far more often than parents believe, the children are aware of the disturbances in the marriage. In such a case, a reference to specific incidents of behavior and the effects upon the spouse or the children and the home life are in order, with the explanation that the separation (divorce) will improve the situation for everyone.

Again, the children should be reminded that both parents love them and the other parent will continue to see and visit them. Sometimes it will be necessary, consistent with the ages of the children, to discuss the economic implications of the divorce and let the children know whether the same or a comparable standard of living will be maintained or not and why and how.

Negative effects of divorce upon children can be substantially mitigated if the mother and father can both explain in the same way. It is the least they owe the children under the circumstances.

It has often been said that children are cruel. Sometimes this cruelty is manifest as other children play with children of divorced parents. Playmates who know that Mary's or Jim's parents are divorced will make remarks to taunt or to hurt the child. What can the mother do? Here again a demonstration of love and affection, and maintenance of a home life with emotional security, can do much toward alleviating the effect of such remarks. The child can be assured that his or her playmates do not understand divorce. The mother can briefly and truthfully explain why the divorce took place. The mother may be able to call the child's attention to other homes where the parents are divorced. The important thing is for the mother to recognize that her child may be unwittingly or otherwise hurt by the remarks of playmates, and to be on guard to provide an environment where her child will be free to talk to her.

In some extreme cases a child might develop psychosomatic symptoms of illness, and therapy at a child guidance clinic may be needed.

The burden is on the mother. Yet, if she made the decision to get a divorce, she must be convinced that her decision was the right one, and that the negative effects on the child if she continued to live with her husband would have been even greater.

Problems of the parent with custody who remarries

Many mothers, recognizing that the children need a day-to-day father figure in the home as well as for personal reasons, accept the idea of a remarriage as a constructive step.

Generalizations are inapplicable to such a decision. The variables inherent in this situation are the age of the mother, the ages of the children, the marital status of the new husband (is he single, widowed, divorced; with or without children; if divorced, does he have custody of his children?) and geography, i.e., where will the new home be? Does the new husband live in the same state, a nearby state, a distant state, or a foreign country?

Many states have statutory provisions forbidding the parent having custody from removing the children from that state without the consent of the court or of the other parent.

Accordingly, when the mother has obtained her divorce and custody of the children in Massachusetts and wishes to marry a man from California and to move there with the children, problems are presented if the father does not agree.

In such cases, if the father does not agree, and application is made for court approval, a hearing is had. The court has jurisdiction over the children and now must consider all factors and decide what is best for the welfare and happiness of the children. In such a case, the court's ultimate decision cannot by definition please all parties.

In one extreme case, the wife and husband were married in 1954 and had two girls, nine and six years of age at the time the case arose.

On November 20, 1962, the wife and husband entered into a separation agreement which among other things provided that for five years from its date, and subject to certain exceptions, the children of the parties were to reside in an area not more than twenty-five miles from Columbus Circle, New York City. This agreement further provided as follows:

> . . . both parties recognize that [the children] are American citizens and children of American citizens and it is their desire that they should be educated within the American school system, and particularly in and about the City of New York. . . .

On January 12, 1963, the wife obtained a divorce in Mexico and the separation agreement was incorporated in and made part of the divorce decree. The children thereafter continued to live with their mother, she having been given custody, with generous visitation rights given to the father.

On November 24, 1965, the mother married her present husband, a natural-born citizen of Israel. The mother had one child by this marriage. On December 7, 1966, the father remarried; his present wife had two children by a prior marriage.

The mother's present husband had been employed by the El Al Israel Airlines for sixteen years and had been assigned to the New York office. He was then reassigned to Israel. If he refused to return to Israel, he would lose his position and all accrued rights and privileges.

The father of the children brought an action in the New York courts to enjoin the mother from removing the children from New York. The court in granting the injunction said:

The court has carefully considered all of the evidence and finds that it is for the best interest of [the children] that they remain here in New York and not be taken to Israel by their mother or her husband. They are American citizens and entitled to be brought up as such. They are entitled to the many benefits that they can receive here, in the land of their birth, which cannot be accorded them in any other country, including Israel. If they went with their mother to Israel, they would in all probability, other than for visits home to see their father, spend the balance of their lives until reaching majority in Israel. By that time they might have so lost touch with the United States that they might decide to remain permanently in Israel. The court has also taken into consideration the unsettled conditions that prevail in Israel today. Although this is a hard decision to make and will mean that the children will be separated from their mother, it is the lesser of two evils and is for the best interests of the children. The respondent mother knew, of course, when she married her present husband that he was a citizen of Israel, here merely by assignment, and that he was subject to recall. As his wife, she will, without cost, be able to make frequent trips to this country to see her children.

This decision of the court should in no way cast any reflections upon either parent. Both parents have demonstrated that they have great love and affection for their two children, and each parent is fully capable of assuming custody of the children under the proper conditions.

A further problem arises when the mother's name is changed as a result of her remarriage. The usual rule is that the children continue to carry their original name. This situation frequently makes for difficulty. In some cases the father will assent to an adoption and change of name by the mother and her new husband. Ordinarily, there will be no change in the name, and this situation must be accepted.

A Bill of Rights of Children in Divorce Actions

Judge Robert W. Hansen of the Family Court of Milwaukee County, Wisconsin, is the author of the following Bill of Rights of Children in Divorce Actions.

 I. The right to be treated as an interested and affected person and not as a pawn, possession or chattel of either or both parents.

 II. The right to grow to maturity in that home environment which will best guarantee an opportunity for the child to grow to mature and responsible citizenship.

 III. The right to the day by day love, care, discipline and protection of the parent having custody of the child.

 IV. The right to know the non-custodial parent and to have the benefit of such parent's love and guidance through adequate visitations.

 V. The right to a positive and constructive relationship with both parents, with neither parent to be permitted to degrade or downgrade the other in the mind of the child.

 VI. The right to have moral and ethical values developed by precept and practices and to have limits set for behavior so that the child early in life may develop self-discipline and self-control.

 VII. The right to the most adequate level of economic support that can be provided by the best efforts of both parents.

 VIII. The right to the same opportunities for education that the child would have had if the family unit had not been broken.

 IX. The right to periodic review of custodial arrangements and child support orders as the circumstances of the parents and the benefit of the child may require.

X. The right to recognition that children involved in a divorce are always disadvantaged parties and that the law must take affirmative steps to protect their welfare, including, where indicated, a social investigation to determine, and the appointment of a guardian ad litem to protect their interests.

Parents, judges, and all interested in children of divorced parents should do everything possible to implement these rights.

CHAPTER VI

In 1966 a dream was realized with the unanimous decision to elect a full-time professional Executive Director of Parents Without Partners, Inc. PWP is the largest organization for single parents. There are chapters in every state in the nation, as well as overseas, working not only with the parents but with their offspring as well.

Mr. Ralph Ober formerly served other volunteer organizations, including the New York Association for Brain-Injured Children. A journalist, he is a former editor of The New York Times, *and has worked for the Associated Press. He is also an attorney and served as an Assistant Attorney-General in New York.*

As Executive Director of Parents Without Partners, Mr. Ober brings a rich experience to the intricate problems of children of divorce.

PARENTS WITHOUT PARTNERS— WITH CHILDREN OF DIVORCE

BY *Ralph Ober*

MARITAL PARTNERS may carry on a running battle for years, filling the house with invective, bitterness, and persistent conflict. Their children are subjected to continual emotional upheaval which varies in intensity from relative calm to open warfare. Many parents who persist under these conditions find personal consolation in the much-abused theory that they are keeping the marriage alive "for the sake of the children."

Such marriages, enduring as they do through tumult and torment, are quite common. Most of them founder along the way, some when the children finally leave the house, others succumbing earlier to the cumulative minor and massive explosions. And there are multi-thousands of marriages which, though wracked with conflict, incompatibility, and irreconcilable differences, go on and on to the bitter end because of religious beliefs, for economic reasons, emotional insecurities, habit, or simply because the marital partners enjoy fighting.

There is no doubt that when parents are unable to resolve their differences even after professional aid, they do great harm to their children by remaining mated "for the sake of the children." Children are far better off living in a one-parent home than with two parents whose marriage has failed. The parents themselves are better off living apart under such circumstances. We shall examine such problems and others in dealing with children of divorce in the following pages.

Marriages are running at the rate of nearly two million a year in the United States. Obviously all couples look forward to a lifetime of happiness and contentment. But, sadly, almost half of these marriages are doomed to failure. Compare the present rate of divorce with that in 1910: then only 87 of each thousand marriages failed; in 1960 one in four marriages broke up. Indeed, we can question the very survival of marriage as an institution.

The average marriage lasts seven years. Six out of seven divorced persons remarry. Nearly half of all remarriages fail again. Two of every three divorces involve children, making more than half a million children affected annually by the breakup of their parents' marriage. It should also be noted for the record that one of every four minor children lives in a home that has been torn by divorce or separation.

These figures are alarming, and become even more so when we realize that the totals are augmented by the addition of some 250,000 unwed mothers each year. It becomes apparent that children of one-parent families are multiplying at an unprecedented rate.

An additional factor which presents itself in the failure of marriage are the common law relationships, now at an all-time high. This condition is largely the result of stringent and archaic divorce laws which, in many localities, limit the grounds for terminating the marriage. Thus, with society-imposed barriers, marriage partners simply leave home to find other companionship outside the bonds of matrimony: an act which is particularly damaging to children and their ideals.

Yet, ironically, even with the odds heavily weighted against a successful marriage, more than 92 per cent of all Americans get married sometime in their life.

The causes of divorce are treated elsewhere and are not within the scope of this study. What concerns us here is the effect of divorce on children. How do we explain to children what is happening in their home? How do we handle young children and teenagers? How should parents conduct themselves toward their children as the marriage nears its end? How can divorcing parents avoid setting off emotional shock waves among their youngsters? How are we to avoid making children pawns of a bitter relationship headed for the courts and possibly newspaper headlines? How do we explain prejudice against children living in split homes? These and related questions face us as we seek to save our children from scars in the battle of the spouses.

Earlier we pointed out that children are far better off living in a one-parent home than in one where their parents are in a chronic state of conflict, discord, or frozen animosity. The reasons are manifest. Bitterness and the eroding influence of a marriage in trouble can only cause anxiety and insecurity in children. The need for the love and understanding of both parents is primary. A study made at Johns

Hopkins Hospital in Baltimore showed that a child's growth and development can be severely stunted as a result of the marital discord of his parents. The report, prepared by four physicians, held that both the emotional and physical development of children is adversely affected in a home beset by parental strife.[1]

Let us examine the case of a young girl whose mother is a member of a chapter of Parents Without Partners, Inc. (PWP), an international organization of single parents and their children. Louise is six years old, the only child of a marriage which ended in divorce after ten years. She had seen her mother suffer a fractured jaw when her father hit her while intoxicated. She had heard her parents scream at one another so many times that she usually appeared to pay no attention to the arguments. She witnessed her mother waving a baseball bat and threatening to beat her father's brains in. She saw the police at the door silencing the couple when the neighbors complained about the noise. But Louise's parents would not break up this insidious marriage simply because "it is far better for the child to have two parents than one." At least that is what a social worker told the child's mother; but ultimately the marriage did end.

Then there are Billy, Debbie, and Susan, whose parents are professionals. Their father is a psychiatrist and the mother heads a secretarial service. The parents are seldom home, each concerned with his own interests and affairs. The parents might be described as being in a perpetually frozen state toward one another, with the freeze slightly tempered for the children. A governess takes care of the youngsters and provides whatever love they get.

A study of the children showed that Billy is excessively belligerent, and rebels both at home and at school. Debbie is overweight and extremely shy, while Susan is ill a good part of the time.

If this family follows the usual pattern, the parents will be divorced when the children are in their late teens or early twenties. Although the children will most likely have had a good education and good marks in school, they will have a hopeless dependency on one or both of the parents. This kind of dependency can well ruin their own marriages because of their deep-seated inability to express love and genuine affection. Their emotions will have been battered. Susan, with her pattern of illness, stands the best chance of responding to early professional help, although the scars of her parents' loveless marriage can remain throughout her life.

Naturally, it is far better for children to live with two parents than with one if the environment is good, one in which the children can experience the security of a contented home. But it is a false assumption that living under the same roof with two parents will always benefit the children. Too many social workers hold this misconception. Where the environment is poor and homelife is filled with tensions, uncertainties, parental absence, or conflict, children do better in a split home. Even when a child appears oblivious to parental strife, one may be assured that its effect is harmful and eroding.

It may prove surprising to some that there are far fewer disturbed children living in split homes than in homes with two parents. Evidence shows that it is the emotional situation at home rather than the parental division which affects a child's adjustment. A child is most disturbed and insecure in a tension-filled home. When the upheaval is resolved, whether by divorce or otherwise, the youngster usually reacts favorably. Remember, children are actually much more adaptable and flexible than adults. This is stressed by J. Louise Despert, M.D., a child psychiatrist and writer.

Dr. Despert writes: "One assurance which modern child

psychiatry can offer parents is that a child can absorb and survive almost any painful experience if he is sure of his family love."[2] Thus, in the stormy period accompanying separation or divorce the child must be made to realize that he is apart from his parents' problems, that he is free to live and love on his own as a person, and that his parents' love for him remains intact and constant. He must know that whatever will happen he shares their unfettered affection, understanding and recognition. He must also know that he is in no way responsible for the strife and the separation which follow. The parents themselves must unreservedly consider first the welfare and interest of their children as they chart a course for divorce. But the sad truth is that in the parental battle for favorable position most adults ignore the rights of their children.

William F. Reynolds, Ph.D., a Professor of Psychology at Queens College in New York and a PWP professional adviser, finds in his experience with children of divorce that fewer suffer from emotional and physical problems than children living in the average two-parent home. "I have observed a healthy adjustment among those youngsters," he told the writer, "especially where their divorced parents do not visit their own bitterness and conflict on their offspring."

This brings us to another manifestation of the effect of divorce on children. It is that children oftentimes instinctively will blame themselves for being responsible for their parents' separation.

Tommy, aged twelve, lived in a household where his father and mother constantly argued. He heard his mother complain about money matters. He heard his father accuse his mother of being a spendthrift. He heard his father accused of infidelity. He saw his father slam the front door many times as he stormed from the house after a bitter dispute. He was privy to arguments in which both parents accused the other of neglecting him. He listened in terror at night from his bedroom while his father said he was leaving the house for good. His mother replied: "God damn you! You can get out and stay out." One day his father left the house for good and a divorce followed.

The sensitive boy blamed himself for the breakup of the marriage. He reasoned that if his parents had not had him around, they would have had no money problems. Both parents used the lad as a sounding board for their own bitterness, and even after the separation, Tommy's mother continued to fill him with the venom she had for her former mate. On the weekends he spent with his dad, the boy suffered through long dissertations on the "vicious woman" he lived with. Such was his custody and visitation life.

It is plain that unless the former partners show restraint and understanding in their relationship with their children, they can fan emotional flames and subject the children to influences which can have very serious effects. In Tommy's case the boy ended up at a psychological clinic for prolonged treatment. Regardless of the severity of the discord, the divorcing parents have an obligation to keep the disease of their own animosity to themselves. When their own love dies, their love for their children must not perish.

What should parents tell their children as a split becomes inevitable? How should parents conduct themselves toward their offspring as incompatibility drives them apart?

If a child has a basic respect for his parent, the separation does not have to be explained in detail. If a child has no respect for his parent as a person, an explanation serves no purpose. The lack of a solid relationship between parents and children may show up most vividly as the parents start to drift apart. If the child lacks respect for his parents, it is clearly an indication that they have been guilty of sheer neglect or just plain ignorance.

Obviously, the age of the children and their degree of comprehension must be taken into consideration when parents decide to talk to them about the impending separation. A very young child would have no idea what it all means. Giving him the reasons for the split would serve no purpose. His needs must continue to be served and he must be assured of the continued love of both parents, whatever the consequences. The comfort, stability, and security of his environment must remain intact regardless of the marital collapse.

But an explanation is due an older child and he should be told simply and honestly, in general terms, the reasons for the marital breakup. He is informed gently and without rancor or bitterness that his parents are going to live apart. He must also be told that they both love him dearly and will continue to love him. He must feel he continues his close and intimate ties with both parents even though they go their separate courses. To avoid emotional shock in their children, adults may want to discuss the problem with a professional or with a member of the clergy. We emphasize again that the welfare and interests of the children must be the primary consideration as the marriage heads for the rocks. Young people require careful guidance and understanding through this significant transition in their lives.

Research undertaken by PWP shows that there is significantly less juvenile delinquency among children of one-parent homes than among those living in two-parent domiciles. This may serve to answer those who feel that young people suddenly thrust into a split home situation may erupt into anti-social behavior. It is true that children of one-parent families face problems at home, in the community and at school as they seek to adjust to a new life, but we may be assured that under ordinary conditions our young people will accommodate themselves very well to the changed environment and will develop normally.

There is a further consideration which may temper some of the fears of those who feel that children uprooted as a result of a marriage failure may be in for greater trouble. Actually, we have found that such children frequently blossom and make great progress as they approach adulthood. Remember that the child in the one-parent home is faced with more responsibilities than those children with two parents. Youngsters will readily assume these responsibilities if they are given the understanding, encouragement, and cooperation of the parents now living apart. But the responsibilities should be outlined clearly and firmly. The need for direction and discipline will persist as the child grows up.

Can a single parent serve as both mother and father to the children? This, obviously, is physically impossible. Yet, single parents frequently seek to fill both roles. It is conceivable that some mothers raising children alone can broil a steak and repair a bicycle. Some can even throw a fair slider. It is possible that some fathers bringing up children alone can bake a cake, sew buttons, and tie hair ribbons. But we must admit there are obvious limitations among the sexes when they invade the areas usually dominated by the other sex.

Yet we know children need both the male and female images. Both are necessary in the maturing process. Where does the missing image come from in the one-parent home environment? Many children of divorce see the missing parent only on rare occasions, in some cases not at all. Some 300,000 desertions are reported annually; in these the second mate has disappeared altogether. The children of unwed mothers do not normally see their fathers. More than a million widows and some 800,000 widowers are raising minor children alone. Where are these children to obtain the missing parent? Are children under such conditions to be raised without the joint benefit of the male and female image?

PWP, a charitable and educational international organization established in 1957, seems to have solved the problem. Substitute mothers and fathers assume the roles of the missing parent. One man may serve as "father" to half a hundred bubbling, noisy youngsters, while one woman may "mother" a busload of children as they go skating or fishing, or as they attend a theatre party, enjoy a teen dance, or go on a picnic or to the movies. The makeshift "moms" and "dads" make up in large part for the missing parent, and they are able to spread their love and affection in generous portions. What this does for the children is heartwarming. The little ones and those who are older actually thrive under such circumstances. As many children ordinarily attach themselves to teachers in school, these similarly evidence their love and devotion to the parent substitute who fills the void in their lives. In a family of more than one child of the same sex it is interesting to note that the children frequently will attach themselves to different adult figures in a PWP chapter.

The substitute mothers and fathers serve as a unique feature of PWP programming for the children. Since all chapters are required to establish a wide range of activities for the youngsters in various age groupings, there are continuing functions for them. When a "father-for-a-day" herds a mass of teenagers into a ball park, he is conducting one of the chapter activities. When a single-parent mom takes a couple of dozen girls to a sewing class, she is doing likewise. The sole "casualties" of this kind of programming are usually the adults, who just cannot keep pace with the energetic youngsters.

Since members stay in PWP for an average of only two years, the question arises, what happens to the social and emotional needs of the children when they are detached from chapter life? The question is usually resolved if the member remarries—and the rate of remarriage in PWP is high. If not, then it becomes necessary to help establish new relationships for the children so that the joint male and female images will not be lost. Some former members thus retain their ties to PWP for the sake of their children. This is possible.

There may be other adult members of the families of single parents who can fill the missing roles—aunts, uncles, grandparents, friends, neighbors. This pool of adults has failed to prove adequate for many single parents, however. But even lacking these aids in the growing-up period, most children will still mature well with the necessary care, love, and domestic direction and discipline at home. But a word of caution: *Do not lend your children your own fears and insecurities.*

We have touched on the great adaptability of children, for as most patients survive the mistakes of their doctors, our little ones usually manage to overcome the emotional stresses imposed by troubled parents and by society itself. But there are many youngsters who are scarred in the conflict of parents, and for these the question arises: Should a parent place a child in therapy?

Observation of children in PWP and from tests conducted in schools would indicate that precipitous action is unwarranted. The professional (psychiatrist, psychologist) usually is the best judge of whether or not to subject a child to psychotherapy. It is the opinion of most of the PWP professional advisers, and of this writer, that parents must exercise great caution against hasty decisions.

There are obviously many situations in which therapy by a competent professional is desirable and can result in much good. But, remember, sending a child for therapy is often a way in which the parent may be trying to avoid his own responsibility and guilt resulting from the dissolution of the marriage. It may make the parent feel better to engage a therapist, thus showing his concern for the child, but oftentimes this benefits only the parent and could have the opposite effect on the child.

The single parent sometimes overreacts to the split-home situation, and he sees demons and hobgoblins in his child. The youngster must be permitted some latitude of reaction over this upheaval in his life, and his behavior might seem strange or different for a time. The parent must be patient in the transition period. Ordinarily the child will settle down and accept the change. One parent we know hurried to school to tell the teachers about her divorce. She wanted them to know that her children now lived in a split home. Was this a good idea?

The simple answer is, no. What is gained by publicly announcing the situation? Nothing, really. The fact that parents need to ask whether or not to let others know about the separation or divorce usually indicates a temporary loss of self-confidence.

Children often pay a high price for psychotherapy. The risk is always there that one might establish a lifelong pattern of dependency and poor self-confidence as a result of ill-advised action. Children of split homes frequently face new problems in the community and at school, but they must be given a fair chance to adjust to their changed conditions. Do not tamper with your child's self-confidence and his abilities. Children prove much stronger psychologically than most people commonly think. A single parent must curb his anxieties and insecurity or he will be provoked into a hasty and unwarranted diagnosis of his child. It is readily acknowledged that the entire question of when to refer a child for therapy is controversial. Many analysts seem to feel that treatment is advisable at the first sign of problems. The more cautious deem otherwise.

Some parents have gone to the extreme of fleeing from a

neighborhood when the marriage fails. As far as the children
are concerned, this is hardly a good idea. The move can
only result in further uprooting and a destruction of ties.
Single parents giving up an old home and a neighborhood
usually are doing so out of their own weaknesses. Their excuse that it helps the children is flimsy. The move simply
forces the children to make new friendships in a strange
environment, to adjust to a different school and new teachers during a time when emotions are still raw and hurt.

Still another problem facing the child of divorce is that of
prejudice. Not only are single parents caught in the web of
social ostracism accorded them as a group, but their children are also subjected to biases of all kinds. Many a mother
living in the "secure comfort" of a two-parent home has told
her Johnny not to play with Stephen who lives in a one-
parent home down the block.

Why? There are some people who feel their children will
become contaminated or tainted if they associate with children of divorce. There are others who harbor the belief that
if they permit their families to become too familiar with the
one-parent home down the block, the "gay" divorcee or the
footloose male might ultimately invade the "secure comfort"
of the two-parent domain. If Stephen's parent is to be kept
away, why just keep Johnny away from Stephen! Prejudice
is hard to fight where it is deeply ingrained. But education
remains the best weapon against it.

The divorced parent frequently becomes prey to the
overly sympathetic neighbor who feels free to offer her un-
solicited advice on how to raise the children. The result is
to further isolate the child of divorce and stamp him as unusual or different in his new role in a one-parent home. The
child should be made to feel no different than the other children in the neighborhood. When the child is made to feel

different from other children, this, too, represents a form of ignorance and prejudice.

And speaking further of prejudice, one would hardly expect it to be flourishing among our institutions of higher learning. Yet it is there, in all its ugly manifestations, where children of one-parent families are concerned. Dozens of colleges and universities across the nation, together with hundreds of private educational institutions, continue to practice an insidious form of prejudice against young applicants of one-parent homes.

We refer to the questionnaires provided prospective students which ask the student about the marital status of his parents. Single parents frequently complain that their children face admission barriers when they answer the question truthfully. Many college admission officials believe that young people from split homes "are less reliable and less able to learn" than those coming from a two-parent family. The admissions officer of a major university in New York State admitted to the writer that the question on the marital status of parents is unfair and prejudicial, but he said the information was important and "helped the college better to understand" the applicant. On pressure applied by PWP, the question was dropped from admission forms of that particular university. But the practice remains widespread.

As this book went to press, PWP had three hundred and fifty chapters located in all fifty states and in Canada. Its membership had grown to 50,000 single parents, all of them widowed, divorced, separated, or unmarried, together with 110,000 children. The tax-exempt, non-sectarian organization had spread overseas, with affiliated groups in England, Australia, and New Zealand.

Besides conducting programs and activities for parents and children, many chapters were concerned with therapy for those adults and young people who needed it. Programs include regional and international conferences with professionally led workshops and outstanding speakers. Most programs are open to the general community, as well as PWP members. All chapters have professional advisory boards, and the international advisory committee is composed of outstanding professionals.

The S.O.S. program seeks, with professional aid, to guide those whose marriages are in trouble. The purpose of S.O.S. is to try to save a failing marriage, if that is possible, or to provide a greater understanding of their problems to those whose marriages cannot be salvaged. Parents enrolled in the five-session undertaking are made keenly aware of the needs of their children, so that if divorce follows, the youngsters will be better off for it. A similar program known as HOW (Help Our Widowed) meets the special needs of widows and widowers. A third program, CRISIS, provides instant help, with the participation of professionals, to those who are new single parents. Again the needs of the children are examined in detail, and help is given during the period when the stress of a split is most acute.

PWP engages in numerous other programs, many of them covering a wide range of subjects especially geared to the single-parent family. Also, a number of research programs have been jointly undertaken with major universities and medical institutions.

CHAPTER VII

"The church must learn to communicate and get to know people in terms of their family crises of conflict and estrangement," says Dr. Wayne E. Oates, Professor of Psychology of Religion and Pastoral Care at the Southern Baptist Theological Seminary in Louisville, Kentucky.

Reverend Oates's concern is the interaction between the pastoral and prophetic ministry of today's Protestant clergyman. He describes how the church can work both preventively and creatively within ecclesiastical tradition to deal redemptively with divorce and children.

The material is garnered from both academic understanding and professional experiences. Reverend Oates has served as minister of urban and rural churches, and as chaplain of general and mental hospitals. He received his Th.D. degree at Southern Baptist Theological Seminary and a Litt.D. at Wake Forest College. He has taught at Wake Forest College, Union Theological Seminary, and Princeton Theological Seminary, and is the author of sixteen books on pastoral care and psychology.

A MINISTER'S VIEWS ON CHILDREN OF DIVORCE

BY *Wayne E. Oates*

WILLIAM L. O'NEILL, in a recent study of divorce, rightly says that "the effect of divorce on children has always been a source of anxiety, but . . . there is little data bearing on the question. . . ."[1] Marriages have often been held together "for the children's sake" upon the advice of ministers who use this argument as the main basis of their appeal. Yet often these ministers' primary motives have actually been to protect their particular convictions that divorce is evil and should be avoided at all costs. If this is the minister's *primary* motive for advising against divorce, then the appeal to the child's welfare is an unintentional but very real use of the child as a means rather than an end. A child can rightly say, then, that he or she is weary of being the *only* cohesive force in a marriage for the sake of the church! My own point of view as a minister is this: A child is a person in his or her own right and should not be used either intentionally or unintentionally as a means for sustaining a marriage. A defective marriage relationship often is made of the same cloth as a defective parent-child relationship.

This chapter is concerned with the communication or explanation of the realities of divorce to the child by the parents and other significant persons around them. Of special interest is the minister's service to the child and his or her parents, or, often, grandparents.

It has been my responsibility as a minister to be a part of the process of interpretation of divorce to growing and grown offspring of divorced parents. The method of discussion here will be to blend a report of the clinical findings in the literature with my own observations as a practicing pastoral counselor.

PROTESTANT CHRISTIAN APPROACHES

Wide variations of thought and practice concerning the pastoral ministry to the family in divorce prevail. In my book *Pastoral Counseling and Social Problems,* I have discussed this in detail. At the outset of this chapter, however, some clear-cut guidance to the family of divorcing or divorced parents with children is needed. What are some of the stumbling blocks to avoid and resources to seek?

First, the Protestant Christian approach depends very heavily upon the personal experience, the training, and the degree of flexibility to be found in the Protestant pastor related to the family. The ideal pastor will take the position of maintaining his relationship of trust and pastoral concern to all members of the family—husband, wife, children, and the in-laws. He will be best equipped to answer the questions of the couple and their children about such problems as Biblical teachings on divorce, whether or not a person who is divorced can be forgiven, whether the act of divorce is the unpardonable sin (it is not!) and how the religious education of the children should best be continued. Unfortunately, the ideal minister is not always the kind of pastor the family has. More than that, the family may feel so alienated from the church and religion by the event of divorce itself that they never give the church a chance to minister to them. Even worse than this, the couple and their children will quite often get their guidance on religion as it relates to divorce from the superstitions of their religiously untrained and even illiterate neighbors and friends.

The good news is that increasing numbers of ministers are being trained to give sympathetic, careful, and wise guidance to their parishioners on the problems of divorce. A common guideline used by these ministers is that every marriage should have an engagement period during which the couple can seek *pre-marital* pastoral care and counseling. Likewise, every potential divorcing couple should have pre-divorce counseling. The couple should not go to the pastor with the expectation that he will "save" the marriage by some magic of words. They should seek his help in learning to communicate with each other and in dealing with the problems of forgiveness and unforgiveness that underly divorce in many instances, and for spiritual and emotional support in time of stress.

One of the ironical things about religion is that it can be a bone of contention between the couple and push them nearer to divorce. This is not only true of the Catholic-Protestant marriage, or of the Jewish-Protestant marriage. It can be true between Protestants, if one partner is extremely zealous in matters of religion and the other indifferent or if one is zealous about one facet of religious beliefs and the other disagrees. Underlying these strains are all kinds of "distance-making" games being played to keep each other apart. To cite an example, I have conferred with couples who violently disagreed on the use of birth control measures though both parties were Protestant. They disagreed for religious reasons.

For many Protestants, the church is an enlarged family. The faithful communicant has not only his "blood-kin" in-laws to cope with in the divorce situation but his spiritual kinsmen in the church as well. Just as in the days of the ministry of Jesus on earth, church people in Protestantism tend to take a variety of stances toward the divorcing couple and their children, the most common being that the Bible says that it is adultery when divorced persons remarry. The next most common stance seems to be that of non-verbal tolerance which leaves the couple in isolation. The purely secular or "civil law" approach to divorce is, regardless of the particular words used, the most influential point of view determining action. As a Protestant minister, I have often been told by lay persons that the church has no business being concerned with the family problems of its communicants! Few are this vocal, but the silent assent is great.

However, the resources of the church in meeting the crisis of divorce focus primarily on the children. If divorce is inevitable, then the church, like the family, tries to pick up the pieces. The child of a divorce who continues to come to the church will tend to be given more special attention and care than other children. The parents of a child should encourage him to have personal conversations with his pastor if he wishes. Ministers of education, directors of Christian education, choir directors, Sunday School teachers, to name a few, provide resources of fellowship in suffering, substitute or rescue parents, and simple but unalloyed friendship. A family not related to a church or a pastor have in an impending or finalized divorce situation a primary reason for seeking out a church and a pastor. A telephone call will often result in a pastoral visit in the home.

One of the great rituals of the Protestant churches is the pastoral call in the home. As a small boy living in a home where my parents were permanently separated, I can remember the awe-inspiring event of a pastor visiting in our home. The Protestant churchman has a *right* to call his pastor. If one proves inadequate, or does not respond to the request for a visit, then he can call another one who will. Protestants are not unique in their emphasis upon pastoral calling, but they *have* established it as an expected ritual in the pastor-parishioner relationship. The pastor, with his training in the Biblical teachings, can clear up many superstitions; he can also introduce the family members to other people their age. He can help them manage the fragile relationships of the family and at the same time assure them that marriage is not the ultimate value in life, although it is as important a proximate human value as any we experience.

THE PROCESS OF MARRIAGE BREAKUPS

The breakup of a marriage ending in divorce is a process from subtle, almost unidentifiable beginnings to a jagged grief situation. Divorce was once one of the luxuries of the middle class. Like retirement, however, it is becoming more widespread among the lower classes. The "poor man's divorce" is desertion, yet, with the passing of the depression of the thirties and the coming of an era of affluence, divorce

is becoming more of a possibility to more people. Consequently, the *other* problems of the more affluent middle and
upper classes hasten to complicate the problem of divorce
and its effects upon children. For example, the dividing of
property, the support of the child, the loss of social-class
status symbols such as club membership, camp opportunities, and even acceptance in a religious group, are more
significant for the affluent family than for the poor. Among
the poor, being on welfare, having no defense in case of
delinquent behavior, and the rapid turnover of "parents"
tend to be the focus of the child's anxiety.

Yet, rich or poor, the process of marital discord which
precedes divorce moves through a similar process. The
communication of the distress to the child varies in manner
and content from one stage to the next. I have identified
these stages as follows:

*Stage 1: The rejection of the ordinary disciplines of mar-
riage.* Here the husband and wife separately or together may
at the outset like each other very much. Whether they *feel*
amorously toward each other is not the issue. The real issue
is whether they have the capacity to change their habit system so that it includes another person at all times. For example, does the husband feel any need to keep his wife
advised of his whereabouts, his schedules, and his activities?
Or, does the wife feel that it is an insult to her professional
integrity to give up her work long enough to have a child
and bring him up to the age where he is able to be at home
with other people? Or, is this more of a "room mate" relationship than it is a covenant of communication and love
between husband and wife?

The child that is born into a home where the necessary
disciplines of marriage are not commonly accepted and
practiced is in itself a threat to the marriage. The development of a commonly understood routine, the clarification of

the "place" or "role" of the woman and the man, the development of good communication, and the "putting away of
childish things" are some of these disciplines. These disciplines when accepted are actually ways of preparing a
home for the coming of a child. If these preparations have
not been largely completed, the coming of a child into the
home brings to the surface tensions that had until then been
ignored. With a child in the home, these disciplines can no
longer be ignored. At the very outset, the child embodies all
these disciplines. Little wonder that Edmund Bergler, a
psychiatrist who wrote a book, *The Children of Divorce,*
found that the child felt deeply that it *caused* the divorce.
The child's very presence "calls the hand" of the husband
and wife who have previously acted as if they were complete
exceptions to the ordinary demands of any marriage. The
minister, lawyer, grandparent, or other person who is in the
position to advise couples contemplating divorce should
focus the attention, not on "saving the marriage" for the
children's sake, but on the risks of the couple's bringing
more children into a home where the ordinary demands of
any marriage are neither accepted nor considered seriously
enough to reach the level of open rejection.

*Stage 2: The stage of the broken covenant and shattered
trust.* Up to this point, the conflict between husband and
wife has been a serious but manageable kind of conflict. The
conflict becomes unmanageable when one or both partners
does, says, or thinks something that the other considers to
be an intentional betrayal of the marriage vows. Conflicts
arise from deception about money, other partners, or even
about who is first in their lives. For example, a couple married previously, divorced, and remarried begin to have serious conflict when their children by another marriage come
first, last, and always. Or when one partner discovers that
the other has a prison record and cannot contract for a

house. Or a wife blandly tells her husband that she has not
been in touch with another man, only to have her husband
discover that she has actually been making a considerable
number of long distance telephone calls to the man.

Betrayals of this kind do not have to be told directly to
the child. He has overheard the heated arguments and draws
his own conclusions as to what has happened. If he feels
guilty about something he has done, he might assume that
this is the cause of the trouble. If the child is present when
physical violence takes place, he or she is pushed into the
position of "taking sides" and protecting the parents from
each other. This protection can go as far as murder. It is rare
for a child to kill a parent, but happens often enough to be
recorded. As a minister, children have called me late at
night to come and help them calm their parents down after
a heated argument.

At this level, the child learns more from "hearing with
his eyes" than he does from having things "explained" rationally to him. The *nonverbal* dimensions of learning are
far more important to him or her than the verbal explanations. The child who grows to maturity and says that he
"never heard his mother and father say an unkind word to
each other" is not saying that they have not *had* sharp disagreements and conflicts. He is saying that they were wise
enough to argue when he was not around.

Yet people usually do not have the control, even if they
have the wisdom, to iron out their differences as husband
and wife at times and places where the child is not exposed
to the conflict. J. L. Schulman writes from tape recordings
of children's interviews with him of how *they* heard the arguments at home. One mother called the father a "philan-
dering scarfaced drunk," the father in the same case called
the child a "little punk," and the mother threatened to kill
the father.[2]

If parents could only put themselves in the child's place—smaller, more uninformed, frightened, and defenseless—then some modulation of their arguments might take place. Yet the most self-indulgent parent, who never controls his or her emotions, tends to be the one who becomes sentimental and wants to "save the marriage for the children's sake."

Stage 3: The stage of withdrawal of selves and silent despair. At this stage the defense systems of both husband and wife move toward personal survival in the face of massive destructive emotions. It becomes safer and easier on everyone concerned to remain silent. There is a blackout of communication, and the playing of marital "charades." This might be called the stage of "private misunderstanding." The couple cannot communicate with each other; yet they have not chosen to talk with anyone outside the family. The child is deeply affected here, because the spouses are tempted, and in many cases succumb, to "using" the child in various ways. Judson Landis lists some of the ways that parents "use" the child: to get information about the other spouse, to arbitrate disputes between the spouses, and to isolate the other spouse by having nothing to do with him.[3] This traumatizing of the child seems to begin the stage of the couple's withdrawing from each other and depending on indirect, nonverbal means of "getting their messages" back and forth.

The damage to the child can be minimized at this stage if the couple will seek outside marriage counseling to lessen the need for "using" the children to be message bearers, arbitrators, and combatants in the conflict.

The reason for this is clear in terms of the needs of the child. At this stage of marital conflict, the first major adjustment has to be made. Now things are different. As Graham B. Blaine, Jr. says, "Children, particularly those younger than ten, can put up with more family discord without being distressed than most adults realize."[4] But when this conflict is smoldering, dishonest, and manipulative, and operates outside an underlying understanding of trust, openness, and frankness, the child begins to realize that it might result in a separation. When the *possibility* of separation or divorce dawns on the child, he has made his first major adjustment. He is filled with the fear of the unknown and the anticipatory anxiety it involves.

The parents who have a minister, priest, or rabbi can serve the best interests of the child by ventilating some of their distress to their spiritual director. The minister or some of his associates usually has access to the child. A public school teacher can fortify the child as divorce becomes imminent. A Scout leader, church school teacher, youth group leader, or even a nearby neighbor can often be a trustworthy listener, a healing presence, a steadfast friend to the child. Much of this can take place nonverbally, without much intellectualization. The important thing is that the child feel that there are people whom he can rely on not to leave him or to use him but to love him for his own sake.

Stage 4: The public phase, or the phase of social involvement. When either the parents or the child or all of them move to some person outside the family to describe their distress, the community as a whole becomes involved. The conflict is no longer a private misunderstanding. In-laws, other relatives, professional counselors, neighbors, and even casual acquaintances become involved in one way or another. They become a part of the problem and, hopefully, a part of the solution.

The particular trauma to the child here arises out of the change in his status in the eyes of both the adults around him and other children or young persons his age. The middle class value of "what-other-people-think" becomes intense. The lower class child may subtly "use" this status to survive both economically and socially. He is likely to get more "sympathy" from public school teachers, church people, and others than the child who comes from a reasonably happy home. The younger the child is, seemingly, the more sympathy he elicits.

Landis discovered that children from the ages of five to eight at the time of the divorce tended to feel more secure, to rate themselves as happier, to be less aware of personal conflicts, and to have fewer feelings of inferiority than any other age group. However, Blaine points out that if the adolescent from twelve to eighteen loses the parent of the same sex, the important task of forming an independent and individual identity is made all the more difficult.

Therefore, the parent of the opposite sex who has the custody of the child can be well advised to have strong and effective persons of the same sex accessible to the teenage child. This can be a minister, a club leader, a school teacher, an athletic coach. The lay religious leader provides a "natural" person for such a task. The divorced person is, in his or her own way, a *widowed* person. The child of divorce in the custody of the mother is a fatherless person in a real way. As times goes on the father is often disengaged from the day-to-day life of the child. Someone must fill this void. The *Epistle of James* describes pure religion in terms of the care of widows and orphans in their affliction.

The social worker's concept of the "rescue family" is a secular correlate of this basic religious injunction. The purpose and function of the church as a social as well as a religious institution is to "fill up the empty places" in people's lives. Blaine goes so far as to say that if the right "identification figure cannot be included in the plans for the placement of a twelve- to eighteen-year-old, then divorce should be postponed if at all possible."[5] His suggestion, from an empirical point of view, is somewhat visionary in the light of the kinds of irrational thinking involved in the process of divorce. A better suggestion would point to *where* the right kind of identification figures can be found. The organized community of the church is such a place. Yet, my own suggestion that the church has this to offer the children of divorce is in itself somewhat visionary, too. The church which has this intention in its conscious mission in the world is rare indeed. The church should, however, have a quiet strategy for meeting the deprivations caused to children and young people by the reality of divorce.

The stage of social involvement is often touched off by the involvement of one or both spouses with "another man" or "another woman." One parent may tell a child about an impending divorce by telling him or her about the "other woman" or the "other man." The child may inadvertently come upon a parent with the third person. Such eye-witness contact makes the child a prime witness in later court proceedings. In my own opinion, the involvement of the child in the legal proceedings, in which he or she is forced to choose loyalties, is one of the most devastating experiences that a child can be exposed to. The divorcing couple should retain one vestige of cooperation with each other in a common vow that the children will not be used this way.

Stage 5: The stage of separation or threat of separation. From the child's point of view, divorce does not mean that an irreconcilable conflict is being settled. It means that one or the other parent is *leaving* him. The feeling of being left, deserted, forsaken is anxiety-provoking to a degree akin to losing someone by death. Divorce focuses the universal fear in mankind, *the dread of abandonment.* The most common reaction to abandonment is one of *idealization* and *self-condemnation.* As Gregory Rochlin says, concerning one little girl, the child "reviles and attacks herself, feels that she is worthless, hates herself, and develops a common type of defense wherein the mother is depicted as excessively good and the child as correspondingly bad."[6]

Another common reaction is *apathy*. The pain of loss and separation may be so great that the only effective way to deal with it is anesthetize it. Of course, numbness and apathy represent one phase of any grief reaction, no matter what the loss may be. However, the child may become fixed at this phase. The parent who observes the child going about life as usual may mistake this apathy for proof of the rightness of the divorce action. To the parents, divorce was an *answer* to their worry about the children. In fact, they may be right. However, the parent would do well to confer with persons who are close to the child outside the home. Even in the home where divorce is not a problem, the parent can often learn much about the inner world of the child by talking with the school teacher, the minister, the Scout leader, the neighborhood house worker. The other children or young persons to whom the child is closely related often know him in ways an adult cannot. The child of divorce may refrain from discussion of his own feelings for the very reason that he knows that the subject is painful to his parents.

The absence of this kind of knowledge of their own children among divorcees may be one of the reasons that Goode found in his study of divorced women that *"92% of these remarried mothers thought that their children's life had either improved or stayed the same.* Only 8% thought that their life had become worse."[7] These mothers may have been out of touch with their children's inner feelings. The children may have been deliberately withholding their innermost thoughts, perhaps even from themselves. During counseling with young people in college and graduate school, many of their feelings come to the surface: fear of abandonment, fantasies about the return of the parent who left the home, and repressed feelings of deprivation, resentment, and loneliness. Not the least among these feelings is the active fantasies that tend to grow up around the event. Here is a list of some of these fantasies, gathered from the conversation of one counselee:

> I knew in my mind that my father had been unfaithful to my mother. This was reinforced not only by what she told me but by what other people told me. But in my daydreams as a little boy, I would imagine that none of this was really so and that he would return one day to look after me and my mother. All this daydream came crashing in when I went to my father's funeral when I was 17 years of age.

> I used to lie awake at night and think that strange noises I heard were actually my father trying to break in the house and to steal me away to be with him. These imaginings continued until I went to school and then I would imagine that this or that teacher would be the kind of man I would find if I really knew my father. I refused to believe in my heart the bad things that people said about my father though I now have enough objective evidence to know that he was indeed an unfaithful husband.

Another set of fantasies grew up in the same counselee's mind:

> I was the youngest child. I often feel that I was the "straw that broke the camel's back" of my parents' marriage. I think that my father took one look at me and left home forever. Maybe if I had not come along they would not have divorced.

> Though I never saw my father but twice in my life, I have trouble listening when anyone says anything harsh about him. I feel the need always to make excuses for him so that people would think highly of him.

This particular counselee never expressed any of these things to his mother, but always sought to be a "model son" for her. Little wonder is it, if we should suppose that this mother was one of the 92% in Goode's sample, that this child would *seem* to his mother to be "better off" or "the same" after the divorce. What appeared as apathy or "adjustment" was a "sealed over" set of active fantasies, an inner world of his own.

Stage 6: The legal phase of the divorce process itself. When divorce procedures are instituted legally, the child faces a fresh set of trauma. That which was threatened in argument or discussion now becomes action itself. The problem focus for the child is the custody arrangements and the certainty of being supported financially. Divorce is expensive. When a couple decide they can *afford* to support two families, this means that they are committing themselves to a double input of time and money. This reality in itself has been an unspoken deterrent to many divorce actions. Where the divorce action is completed and not deterred, this reality becomes a shaking disillusionment to parents who thought they would "never have it so good" and that all their problems were caused by their marital situation.

One determinant of the degree and kind of effects upon the child is whether or not the parents plan to remarry. The presence of an adult man in the home and the security of a place that is *home* provide crucial nutrients in the psychological security of a child. For example, one counselee lived securely with his mother, though she had to go to work, from the age of seven until she remarried when he was fifteen. Uncles provided security for him as identification figures. At the time of remarriage, his mother decided that he should go and live with his own father. This began a long tortuous journey of going from one to the other. Each move was prefaced by a quarrel with the parent he was with at the

time. As he entered graduate school, he was still torn between the two locales. His most recent solution to the
problem has been to deliberately create a substitute home
atmosphere from the new people he has met in the city
where he goes to school.

During the time of the custody "rat race" of part-time
here and part-time there, as Blaine says, "all too often the
children are used unintentionally as pawns in a complicated
power struggle between divorced husband and wife."[8] The
longer-range realism points toward what both parents
should face: *Divorce ordinarily means that the child will
sooner or later lose touch with one or the other of his parents.* Therefore, if a clean-cut decision about which relationship will be lost were made a part of the divorce agreement
at the outset, the long-range benefits to the child would be
more secure. Probably in most instances this means that the
father not only "pays through the nose" financially for a
divorce; he also pays similarly from an emotional point of
view in giving up his children. But whether the sacrifice is to
be made by the mother or the father, a clean-cut break made
with as little sentimentality as possible in the long run contributes to the well-being of the child.

When this cannot be effected, usually the arrangements
of courts are week-end visiting, vacation visiting, summer
visiting, half-time with one parent and half-time with the
other, and so forth. At best, these tend to become less and
less tenable with the passing of time. The child develops
friendships with other children, gets a program of activities
and a schedule of his or her own, and more and more the
visits with parents become contrived and unnatural. The
topics of conversation become less varied. Day-to-day fellowship with a child is a natural prerequisite to comfortable
conversation. Similarly from the parent's side, he or she

develops new interests, relationships, and schedules. Often promises are made that cannot be fulfilled.

My own suggestion to parents at this point is that the child's own well-being must be the main criterion and not the desire of the parent to prove something. The child's desire, especially in the instance of older children, should be consulted. Promises should be conservative and fulfillment liberal. In other words, one should always promise less than he delivers. Likewise, to include other children who are playmates on outings eases the pressure of the child feeling that he or she must go through the motions of talking adult conversation with an adult. Particularly is this true of preadolescent and early adolescent children. Their chums tend to take precedence over their involvement with parents. In short, the divorced parent is under obligation, even more than other parents, to take seriously the kinds of demands that *any* child makes upon any parent, quite apart from the factor of divorce.

Stage 7: Post-divorce grief. The experience of losing someone by divorce is a jagged grief experience. Often, persons in the process of divorce will say that they could have dealt with the whole break much more easily if their partner had died. This identifies the experience as a grief situation and underscores the death wish that is felt toward the marital partner. Grief ordinarily goes through several phases itself: shock, numbness, a struggle between fantasy and reality, periods of extreme despair and depression, times of selective memory, and the reconstruction of life around a new love object. In the grief process, especially when we lose someone by death, we usually repress and deny all negative feelings we have toward the deceased. We tend to idealize him and even deify him. However, in the grief process after a divorce, the process works in just the reverse manner; we repress and deny all the positive feelings we have and tend to vilify and derogate the former mate.

The parent in this vilification and derogation is likely to do the most damage to the child. The damage is a double harm: the parent (1) destroys every good impression the child has of the other parent, and (2) creates a credibility gap between himself and the child. The child's experience of the other partner may be very different. For example, an alcoholic husband may have had a very poor relationship with his wife and, to the contrary, be somewhat sentimentally and tenderly related to his child. Furthermore, as the child, even in the face of the truth of what the parent says against the other parent, recreates a positive identification with the other parent, he will tend to reject the wisdom of the parent who did the vilifying. This will particularly be true if the step-parent who takes the place of the divorced parent is for any reason unacceptable to the child as he or she grows from childhood to maturity. The judgment of the parent in choosing such a replacement for the original parent is questioned, and the credibility gap is complicated with resentment that the parent now puts the new spouse in the place of affection that the child himself or herself filled before this second marriage.

Therefore, the parent who is divorced only does himself or herself harm in the eyes of the child when this vilification and derogation take place. Everything should be done to sustain as good an image of the divorced parent in the mind of the child as is possible without "leaning over backwards" to distort the truth in the other direction. After all, the partner doing the disparaging of the other *chose* that partner for marriage, to engage in loving intercourse with, and to help bring this child into the world. Completely to reject the divorced parent is to reflect on one's own judgment rather poignantly at the most crucial level for the child.

All of us have sinned, and like sheep have parted each one to his own way. Forgiveness is rarely mentioned in the discussion of divorce, but confession and forgiveness can, within certain general outlines, be the emotional tone and stuff of the conversation of the parent with the child about the other parent. Ministers can firmly but gently encourage the maturity of "children of divorce" by encouraging them to accept both parents as human and *not* divine. He can help lower the somewhat unrealistic expectations that all children tend to have of their parents. A careful and leisurely exploration of the ambiguities of the data about his or her parents the child has in mind will aid this process of forgiveness.

Stage 8: Remarriage. Jessie Bernard rightly points out that remarriage of divorced persons is the patterned norm today and not the exception. In a summary of data on divorced men and women who had children, the balance leaned slightly in the direction of a favorable, friendly, affectionate, and accepting relationship between the children and the new parent.[9] About 84 percent of divorced persons remarry within 14 years. One out of three remarriages of divorced persons will end in divorce again, but a little over half of these marriages are as happy or happier than the marriage of persons who have been married only once. There is at least one child involved in the average remarriage of divorced persons.

My own pastoral counseling experience points to several factors that lead to happiness and to unhappiness in children of remarried divorcees.

FACTORS LEADING TO HAPPINESS

Adequate introduction, time for getting acquainted, and care in developing a relationship between the children and the new spouse that is consonant with the relationship between their mother or father and the new spouse.

A clear definition of the lines of authority in the discipline of the child, and a subsequent maintenance of these lines with consistency.

A happy and relaxing sexual relationship between the new husband and wife. This removes any overdevelopment of erotic needs between the new parent and the children of the other spouse. It removes much of the rivalry particularly on the part of teenage daughters with their mother for the new stepfather's attention, or between the teenage sons and their father for the stepmother's attention.

FACTORS LEADING TO UNHAPPINESS

Any of the same factors that led to the breakup of the first marriage and which are obvious enough for the children to identify in the new marriage.

Failure to establish the kind of relationships described above.

A conscious choice on the part of the parent of the child to place the child above the need to cooperate as husband or wife with the new spouse. This can be spoken in the hearing of the child and the new spouse and lay the groundwork for wrecking the new marriage.

A competition on the part of the children for maintaining the "place" they had when they had the parent to themselves. In other words, they never "make room" for the other spouse in the home.

An abdication of the parental role by the new spouse and a relegation of these responsibilities to the parent of the child.

Crucial Concerns of Children of Divorce

The process of divorce and the corresponding involvement of the child have been discussed. The parents of the child, the minister of the child, and the other adults significantly related to the child need to understand his struggles to better equip them in conversations with him.

First, the child "knows," has much more intuitive, anxious unspoken skills than do the adults around him. The assumption that he or she is too young to know much about it is an adult judgment. The child has a "feel" for what is happening but lacks objective information. The parents should at least agree on how to provide basic information to the child.

Second, the child observes with all his or her capacity that *trust* has gone out of the relationship between the parents. "Trust" is Erik Erikson's term for what the religious persons call a personal faith. The minister and the lay people of the church walk a narrow ridge between "taking over" in the whole relationship of the child and "playing hands off" altogether. A balanced approach is needed to strengthen the child's confidence in himself and his parents and at the same time encourage the child to make a life for himself apart from the conflicts of his parents. The child of divorce has to "leave father and mother" emotionally much earlier than the child from an intact family. This makes him grow up earlier. Divorce demands putting an "old person's head on a young person's shoulders." Religious faith can nourish some of the frustrated and deprived but legitimate needs for dependence in the child.

Third, the child of divorced parents is often forced to compensate for his or her frustrations and deprivations by excelling in areas where he or she *is* competent. Excelling in school work, athletics, drama, making money, and being independent are a few of the socially acceptable compensatory devices. His or her friends mean more to the child. He or she may develop strong motivation for the social sciences that improve family living. Landis's study suggests that the major effect of divorce on children is to make them cautious and "leery" about marriage, and to create in them the resolve to "learn all about it" and insure a successful future home life of their own. Casual inspection of the personal histories of marriage counselors reveals a high percentage of them have themselves come from divorced homes. This author did.

Fourth, all these add up to the crucial tendency of the child of divorce to take too much responsibility for everything. The feelings of guilt that he or she might be "the cause" of divorce is one expression of this. The child's sensitivity to conflict and trouble seems to be much more acute than that of adults. Conclusive data suggest a correlation between divorce and delinquency in children, although the same data suggest that children from homes broken by death are even more prone to delinquency.[10] But the incidence of children of divorce entering the professions of social work, psychology, psychiatry, law, and the ministry has yet to be studied.

Finally, the effect of divorce upon children's religious concern is an unexplored continent for research. Divorced parents often exhibit less adult traits than do their children —no wonder "a little child shall lead them." The child takes too much responsibility for one reason: the adults he knows refuse to take enough. Thus he or she becomes the leader. As weak, alone, inexperienced and afraid as this makes the child, would it not be an hypothesis worth studying to say that the child is prone, to say the least, to search for a stable parenthood in God himself?

CHAPTER VIII

Much has been written about the many changes that have taken place in the Roman Catholic Church. No issues are more controversial than those of the family—contraception, divorce, remarriage.

Father John Lawrence Thomas, S.J., is uniquely qualified to discuss the question of divorce and children in the Catholic Church. He received his Ph.D. degree at the University of Chicago and was a recipient of the Guggenheim Fellowship. A former President of the American Catholic Sociological Society, and Professor at St. Louis University, he is currently Research Associate at the Cambridge Center for Social Studies. Some of his books include: The American Catholic Family; Marriage and Rhythm; *and* Religion and the American People.

A PRIEST'S VIEWS ON CHILDREN OF DIVORCE

BY *John L. Thomas*

WE MAY AS WELL BEGIN by admitting frankly that we really cannot explain divorce to children. The best we can hope to do is to help them come to terms with those consequences of divorce that affect them personally. As adults with some awareness of the difficulties currently associated with achieving successful marital adjustment, we may marvel that so many marriages succeed as well as they do; but children are not likely to share our apprehensions in this regard. They take family life more or less for granted, are equally attached to both their parents, feel the need for their continued loving support, and regard them as models of grown-up perfection. Divorce may mark the legal dissolution of a marriage bond; it does not dissolve these basic parent-child relationships, for they are "givens," rooted in the very nature of things. By breaking up the family circle and consequently the normal basis of family interaction, divorce clearly hinders the development of these relationships; it cannot destroy them.

This serves to remind us that a family is both "covenant" and "community" at the same time. As a union of love involving a couple's freely chosen mutual commitment to a shared existence, it is covenant. As a life-giving, two-in-one-flesh unity involving the concrete givenness of offspring, it is community. Divorce can legally dissolve covenant, for the love underpinning commitment may fail to persist; it cannot destroy community, for the factual basis underlying the parent-child relationship is no longer subject to choice. Especially in a family system built on monogamy, nothing can really destroy the peculiar bonds vitally relating parents and children. One or both parents may accept or reject their children; they cannot dissolve the relationship. Children may love or hate their parents; they cannot ignore them, even if unknown. Young children in particular want parents, dead or alive.

This means that when divorce formally dissolves a family as well as a marriage, it can never be "final," though it may constitute the best available solution once covenant fails or family interaction becomes destructive. In this respect, divorce is only a legal device designed by society to deal with some of the social consequences of marital failure. As such it can solve none of the essentially private, intensely personal human problems resulting from frustrated expectations and unfulfilled shared commitments. Hopefully, however, it may provide the basis for a realistic reappraisal of the situation and a workable restructuring of the relationships that persist. In this sense, as I have suggested, "explaining divorce to children" means helping them adjust to the new situation.

THE EXTENT OF THE PROBLEM

Although we are directly interested here in only some aspects of divorce, a brief overview of our contemporary family system may help us maintain proper perspective. Most Americans appear to be perennial optimists in matters relating to love, marriage, and the family. Compared to their contemporaries in other western countries a greater proportion enter marriage; they marry on the average at earlier ages; and they marry more often. Contemporary family attitudes and practices are largely the result of three major factors: the fairly diverse domestic backgrounds of the early settlers and later immigrants; the influence of a tradition-free, open-class, challenging new environment; and the rapid industrialization of the country, starting after the Civil War and resulting in the family's transition from a primarily rural to an increasingly urbanized social setting.

In spite of their original diversity, American families now appear very much alike in size, structure, and the general patterning of activities throughout their life cycle. Some differences related to various regional, social class, ethnic, religious, and "racial" differences obviously persist, but the basic trend toward uniformity is unmistakable. This trend reflects, in part, the adjustments required by an industrialized urban environment. American families must operate in a technologically advanced, rapidly changing society. For the most part, they are spatially and socially mobile, enjoy relative affluence, and are highly receptive to the uniformities promoted by mass communications. Because they must adjust to roughly similar social environments, they adopt somewhat similar family attitudes and patterns.

Among the more significant features characterizing present thinking about marriage and the family are the belief that young people should be free to select their future partners, that marriage should be based on love, that the marriage bond should be permanent though legal provision should be made for separation or divorce in specified cases, that parenthood should be responsible and therefore somewhat restricted, that newlyweds should establish a household apart from their parents, that grown children should be self-supporting, and finally, that interaction among relatives or the extended family should be founded on affection rather than on a set of formally defined duties and obligations. In contrast to the past, modern couples place greater stress on individual freedom, personal fulfillment, and conjugal companionship. Since these new expectations must be met within the presently narrowed family circle composed only of husband, wife, and children, it is not surprising that the rate of frustration runs high. Even minor misunderstandings or disagreements loom large in this restricted circle, for its structure not only intensifies the emotional content of difficulties when they arise but precludes direct assistance from the wider circle of relatives.

Although available statistics are far from adequate, we can safely estimate that over a half million marriages are annually dissolved by divorce.[1] This means that approximately one out of four marriages eventually ends up in court. Children under eighteen are involved in some sixty percent of these broken marriages, and their custody is given to the mother roughly nine times out of ten. The number of children actually living with only one parent at any given time does not reflect the full extent of the problem, since it is estimated that some four-fifths of divorced men and three-fourths of divorced women will marry again. Recent research in large urban centers indicates that by age eighteen between thirty and forty percent of all children have experienced a home broken by death, divorce, or separation.[2]

To what extent are Catholics involved in marital failure and divorce? Unfortunately, our national statistics are not broken down according to religious beliefs; and as we shall point out, we must rely on limited research and general estimates in this regard. Before presenting what information we have, it may be well to point out that special concern with the nature and amount of family disorganization among members of a religious minority is based on the assumption that a couple's religious convictions will affect their family values, attitudes, and practices to some discernible extent.[3] Specifically, since the Catholic church teaches that marriage is founded on a sacramental contract characterized by perpetuity, indissolubility, and mutual fidelity, and that the family furnishes the only acceptable institution within which couples may fully develop and express their mutual sexual complementarity, it seems logical to assume that the practical implications of this teaching will be reflected in the marriage and family conduct of Catholics.

Considered against the broader backdrop of American religious pluralism, some aspects of the stresses and strains experienced by Catholic couples will appear unique and specific, consequently justifying separate study and analysis.[4] For example, belief in the indissolubility of the sacramental bond should be reflected both in serious intent to preserve marital unity and in refusal to remarry after obtaining a civil divorce. Catholic teaching on the nature and purposes of sex can be expected to influence courtship patterns, as well as attitudes toward infidelity and morally permissible means of family limitation. Interfaith marriages will probably reveal some incompatibility in family goals and standards, with consequent tension and loss of unity. At the same time, the diversity and varied degrees of ethnic solidarity so characteristic of the Catholic minority in this country because of its relatively recent immigrant background may provide added sources of stress and strain in intergroup marriages and even between partners of the same national origin, since the process of acculturation does not proceed uniformly among all members of a given ethnic group.

American Catholic couples may encounter special problems from other sources. They are predominantly urban and consequently experience the full impact of the extensive social changes marking contemporary society. As members of a religious minority embracing a distinctive set of beliefs relating to marriage and family life, they must work out their adjustments within a framework of values, many elements of which are based on theological and philosophical premises not generally accepted in the dominant culture. Since family values have functional demands or exigencies, that is, their continued realization in a given social milieu requires the support of related institutions and practices, Catholic families are subjected to additional strain, for a loosely integrated, pluralist society is likely to furnish little of this requisite support.

Thus, although we may reasonably conclude that Catholic couples are religiously motivated to make a success of their marriage, we should also keep in mind that they may encounter more difficulties than others in trying to live up to the demands of their distinctive religious beliefs under contemporary conditions. If we may judge from the case loads of social workers, the records of marriage counseling centers, the findings of parish surveys, and the testimony of experienced chancery officials and pastors, it appears that Catholic couples are experiencing an increasing amount of marriage and family problems, probably differing very little in this regard from their contemporaries of similar educational and socioeconomic background. There is some evidence that Catholic couples are more likely than others to choose legal separation or desertion rather than civil divorce when seriously disruptive family problems arise. This tendency undoubtedly reflects the church's teaching regarding the indissolubility of marriage; it does not affect the basic conclusion that Catholic couples are evidently experiencing an increasing amount of marital strain and breakdown.

It is not our purpose here to analyze the factors involved in this apparent increase, yet a brief observation seems in order. Past research on family breakdown among Catholics has indicated that when serious difficulties arose, the decision to seek a separation or divorce was not taken lightly in the majority of cases.[5] At least one of the partners was found to regard marriage as the source of serious obligations and commitments binding in conscience. Failure was admitted only when family relationships had either deteriorated to a mere empty shell or become seriously harmful to family members.

Granting that other factors may be operative, it appears that separation and divorce are more frequently chosen nowadays as a solution to family discord because many traditionally conservative lower or middle class Catholic wives are beginning to redefine their status and roles in marriage and the family. The current trend toward greater equality and independence for women, implying as it does a weakening of the foundations upon which the prerogatives of male dominance in marriage were formerly based, has led many wives to be less tolerant and long-suffering than in the past. In contrast to their mothers or grandmothers, modern wives prefer to support themselves and even their children rather than put up with irresponsible, abusive, drunken, or unfaithful spouses. Owing to better education, previous work experience, and the availability of employment, they are less fearful of separation or divorce and may feel that such a solution best serves the real interests of their family. The crux of the problem in this situation is that husbands are

loath to redefine their status and roles. Many Catholic men
in particular proceed on the assumption that their wives will
not leave them; and since they may be conducting themselves about as their fathers did before them, they feel they
are justified.

Do divorced Catholics remarry to the same extent as
their contemporaries in similar circumstances? One would
expect to find some differences in this regard because the
church teaches that a civil divorce does not dissolve a sacramental marriage bond. No reliable information is available
on this important point, though all parish censuses discover a
relatively large number of couples living in marriages regarded as invalid because of the existence of a previous
bond on the part of one or both partners. To understand this
situation it is helpful to note that our contemporary family
system, with its emphasis on the small nuclear or conjugal
family unit, is ill-equipped to reabsorb a divorced member.
The church's teaching regarding remarriage undoubtedly
serves as a powerful restraining force, yet considering the
burdensome problems involved, it seems logical to conclude
that a fair number, particularly of younger divorced Catholics, ignore the Church's sanctions and attempt another marriage.

DIVORCE AND THE LAW

Divorce may be defined as the formal dissolution of an existing marriage bond. Its meaning consequently depends on
what one believes is the meaning of marriage. Inasmuch as
the Catholic church and the various American states define
marriage somewhat differently, it is not surprising to find
that they have a different view of divorce.[6] These differences
merit further consideration because they affect the way Catholics deal with the consequences of divorce. In this respect

it may be helpful to point out that Catholics regard themselves as members of two separate societies—the church or ecclesiastical society, into which they are incorporated through baptism; and the civil society of a given nation or state, in which they acquire citizenship either through birth or naturalization. Their membership in both these societies gives them definite rights and obligations, and it also places them under the jurisdiction of these two different societies in regard to matters pertaining to these rights and duties.

This means that the marriages of Catholics are regulated both by the canon law of the church and the civil law of the state. This dual legal system gives rise to confusion and conflict if church and state do not agree in defining the limits of their jurisdiction in regard to marriage. Such a condition exists in the United States, for the various states claim complete jurisdiction over the marriages of their citizens and thus maintain their right to define the conditions required for a valid marriage, as well as the grounds for its legal dissolution. The Catholic church makes similar claims in regard to the marriages of its adherents, with the result that civil law may accept as valid a marital union that canon law may declare to be null and void, or may legally dissolve a marriage bond that canon law regards as indissoluble.

Briefly, in its code of canon law the church defines its jurisdiction over marriage as follows: "The marriage of baptized persons is governed not only by divine law but also by canon law, without prejudice to the competency of the civil power as regards the merely civil effects of such marriage" (Canon 1016). As gradually developed down through the centuries this power of jurisdiction has come to include the imposition of conditions for the licitness and validity of the contract, the establishment of various impediments to the contract, judicial control over matrimonial cases involving Christians, and the enforcement of marriage laws through ecclesiastical penalties. This jurisdictional power is based on the belief that Christian marriage is a sacrament. According to Catholic teaching, this means that Christ has incorporated the natural institution of marriage into his redemptive plan, using it as a special means through which Christian husbands and wives are brought into redemptive union with him and sanctified for their distinctive mission among the people of God.

Because of this belief, Catholics maintain that the state has no jurisdiction over the validity of a marriage contract between Christians, though it does have the right to make reasonable regulations relating to marriage licenses, health tests, public records, and the civil effects of the contract. In both church and state legal codes the marriage contract is defined as *sui generis;* that is, it differs from all other contracts in the sense that neither the basic mutual rights and obligations it involves nor its duration are determined by the contracting parties. In the practical order this means that marriage partners must accept the essential contents of the contract as defined in law, and they are not free to terminate the contract at will or by mutual consent. The state bases its authority in this regard on the argument that since marriage involves significant public interests, the conditions governing its formation and dissolution must be regulated by civil law and subject to judicial decision.

Although the church teaches that a validly contracted and consummated marriage between baptized Christians can be dissolved only by the death of one of the partners, its canon law does provide for "incomplete" divorce or legal separation, which grants spouses the right to cease cohabitation (separation *a mensa et thoro,* from bed and board, as opposed to separation *a vinculo matrimonii,* from the bond of marriage). This permission is given when the good of one or both the spouses or of the children requires it. Since relatively prolonged or permanent separation also involves a redefinition of important rights and obligations, couples are usually granted permission to obtain a decree of separate maintenance or divorce from the civil courts. This has led to some misunderstanding in the popular mind. Although divorced, such separated spouses remain in good standing within the church, provided, of course, they do not attempt another marriage.

A further point of confusion regarding the church's teaching calls for some clarification. The code of canon law establishes a rather elaborate system of "marriage" courts.[6] For the most part, these courts are concerned with cases in which the validity of a marriage contract is at issue or a dissolution of an existing marriage bond is sought. The validity of a given marriage bond may be challenged if there is evidence that the conditions required for making a valid contract were not fulfilled. If this can be proved to the court, a declaration of nullity is granted. Although such a declaration is popularly termed an *annulment,* this is a misnomer. The court does not nullify or dissolve an existing valid bond in this case; it merely declares, on the basis of the evidence presented, that what purported to be a valid marriage was invalid from the beginning.

Contrary to what is commonly believed, church legislation does provide for the dissolution of a valid marriage bond under certain clearly defined conditions—legitimate annulments. Thus, for serious cause, a valid, sacramental (between baptized persons) *unconsummated* marriage, as well as a valid, consummated *non-sacramental* (one or both partners unbaptized) marriage, may be dissolved; and the parties to the contract are free to marry again. Because of the conditions required (the marriage must be either unconsummated or non-sacramental), however, the annual number of such cases is relatively low. I have called attention to this procedure only to clear up some common misconceptions. The church's marriage courts deal primarily with cases involving doubtful validity of the contract, not annulment of an existing bond; though church law does provide for the true dissolution of a valid marriage contract in some instances. According to the code of canon law currently in effect, of course, a valid, consummated, sacramental marriage is held to be terminable only with death. Separation is permitted in some circumstances, but neither separation nor civil divorce can dissolve the marriage bond.

One further comment on divorce and the law is relevant to our discussion. Although only Catholic couples face the somewhat perplexing condition of having their marriages regulated by two different legal codes, a glance at the divorce laws and practices of the various states reveals a much more puzzling situation. In theory, divorce can be obtained only as the result of a court fight; that is, through an adversary proceeding designed to establish the "guilt" or "innocence" of the defendant. A divorce decree is granted if the defendant is found guilty of one of the grounds defined by the law of the particular state as a cause for divorce, and if the plaintiff is innocent of any such charge. But in practice, about ninety per cent of all divorces are uncontested. This means that in the great majority of cases the "guilt" of the defendant is admitted without being contested, and the essential questions regarding property settlement, custody of the children, and support are settled by the partners extrajudicially through their lawyers. Contrary to legal theory, the courts merely rule on the technicalities of the divorce.[7]

In this anomalous situation there is little assurance that legal justice will be done and the rights of all adequately protected. Once divorce proceedings are initiated, the partners are almost wholly at the mercy of their lawyers in regard to both the formulation of the legal grounds for action and the kind of separation agreement they are able to negotiate. Often a feeling of helplessness, together with the desire to get the painful proceedings over with as quickly as possible, leads to hasty compromises and imprudent decisions having long-range consequences for the welfare of the participants. Particularly if one of the partners is eager to obtain the divorce, concessions relating to custody or support may be made that later prove quite unrealistic and become the source of frustration and resentment. Yet, unless the terms of separation agreements are very obviously impractical or unjust, the courts tend to accept them, owing to lack of time and the absence in most parts of the country of any judicial machinery capable of investigating a total marriage situation. Moreover, in the roughly one out of ten cases in which the divorce is contested, the ensuing court fight tends to be unduly prolonged, humiliating, and costly.

I have called attention to this publicly recognized yet tolerated gap between the legal superstructure and the frequently collusive, semi-bootleg procedures characterizing actual practice because it best illustrates the ambivalent feelings about divorce found in contemporary society. Most Americans feel that since marriage is a private, personal affair, if a marriage fails, the couple should be able to obtain a divorce with a minimum of interference from society. At the same time, they disapprove of divorce as a solution for marital conflict, assume that someone must be at fault when a marriage fails, distrust divorced persons to some degree, and in general, regard divorce as a social deviation that really shouldn't occur and that therefore should be treated as something exceptional. As sociologists would say, divorce is not fully institutionalized in American society. Although divorce has become prevalent, society has not yet developed an appropriate set of legal, judicial, and social procedures for dealing with it.[8] For its part, the church has a clearly prescribed mode of official behavior for handling cases of marital failure and separation, but it has shown little positive concern in dealing with the practical consequences of its official position under contemporary conditions.

THE MEANING OF DIVORCE

Divorce is the legal dissolution of a marriage or family, and as such, it is a purely legal affair. But neither marriage nor divorce occurs in a social vacuum. Their real meaning derives from the total cultural context within which couples enter marriage, start their families, encounter marital difficulties, get a divorce, and attempt to restructure their lives. For this reason it has been necessary to call attention to the wider social, legal and religious frameworks of beliefs, values, attitudes, and normative practices relevant to marriage and divorce in our society. As I have noted, "explaining divorce to children" means helping them come to terms with the consequences of divorce as they personally experience them. These consequences will necessarily be related not only to their previous experience of family life and the adjustments required by the dissolution of this way of life but also to the attitudes and actions they encounter in others as children of divorced parents. Divorce has meaning for children to the extent that it modifies their immediate family relationships, as well as the social climate of opinion within which they are growing up. This latter is so important because it affects the child's sense of security and concept of self.

Other contributors to this volume have amply treated the significance of previous family experience. It should be obvious that this will be a minor item for the very young child and a negative experience for the child who fears or dislikes the departed parent.[9] If family life was marked with constant quarreling, tension and strain, divorce may even be regarded as a positive gain. There is indeed considerable evidence to suggest that growing children find such stressful family situations much more difficult to understand and cope with than the actual loss or departure of one of the parents.[10]

Other contributors have discussed the varied and relatively wide range of possible practical problems that may be consequent on divorce and the attempt to maintain a one-parent family. These will differ according to the sex, age, and number of children, the economic or financial resources available, the sex of the remaining parent, and the social class of the family. Most of these practical problems are not specific to one-parent families resulting from divorce but are usually encountered by families broken by the death or prolonged absence of one of the parents.

Since a large proportion of divorced persons in our society eventually remarry, the very human problems associated with integrating a new parent into the family circle have also been discussed by other contributors. These problems will, obviously, differ with the age and sex of the child, the quality of the child's attachment to the parent who is being replaced, and the extent to which the closeness of the parent-child relationship achieved in the one-parent situation appears to be threatened by the introduction of a significant new member into the family circle.[11] Children of divorced Catholics who remarry face additional problems, of course, for their parents are excluded from active participation in the sacramental life of their church, and children may find this difficult to understand or explain to their peers, particularly if they are attending parochial school and acquiring a vivid awareness of what the church teaches in this regard.

The meaning of divorce for the partners also depends on their previous experience in marriage, the adjustments involved in restructuring their separate lives, and the reactions they encounter in others.[12] As a general rule, marriage breakdown is a gradual process in which one or both parties find adjustment progressively more difficult and eventually decide to terminate the relationship by divorce. Although the initial experience of marriage may have been relatively satisfactory, by the time the decision to dissolve partnership is reached, the marital relationship has probably become a source of painful frustration rather than positive, personal fulfillment. The dissolution of a marriage that has endured any length of time necessarily involves suffering, for cherished hopes have been destroyed, and serious commitments unfulfilled. Publicly exposed failure is always difficult to bear, while fruitlessly sacrificed lifetime, love, and intimate concern—"the best years of my life"—are bound to generate some bitterness and resentment.

The dissolution of marriage does not return the partners to the premarital state of singlehood. Their lives have been mutually geared to reciprocal intimacy, the maintenance of a common enterprise, and a shared destiny. Restructuring their lives after divorce requires not only the readjustment of routine daily relationships but the formulation of new life-goals and aims. Because children and parent-child relationships remain as "givens," they impose both material and psychological limits to the solutions available. In most instances, mothers are given custody of the children, but fathers are generally held responsible for their support; and no solution ever frees either parent from the peculiar bond of parenthood.

As I have mentioned, public reaction to divorce is ambivalent. Divorced persons frequently find that the very relatives and friends who counseled them to seek a divorce, later regard them with some distrust or suspicion. In our thoroughly couple-centered society the divorced are "extras" in social life and "exes" regarded as a potential threat to the currently married wherever they are. Because divorce is not fully institutionalized in our culture, people are not taught how to deal with the divorced, and the divorced themselves are not sure how they should behave. As a matter of fact, society in general is uneasy about them and feels much better (or safer?) when they remarry. Well-intentioned relatives and friends may frequently try to promote remarriage, apparently on the assumption that one ought to be married and that any marriage is better than none. This implicit mistrust or concern may add to the problems of readjustment, for it may further undermine the divorcee's self-confidence and expose her to painful encounters with shallow "friends" mistakenly confident that they can fulfill her imagined needs.

Explaining Divorce

My approach in this paper has been based on two assumptions: first, that explaining divorce to children means helping them come to terms with the consequences of divorce as they personally experience them; second, that parents teach primarily by what they are rather than by what they say. Most of the routine, practical consequences of divorce are fairly obvious though highly variable, and other contributors have already discussed them satisfactorily. However, since my primary concern here is with the special problems encountered by Catholic couples, my second assumption needs further development in their regard.

As I see it, besides providing for the normal physical, affective, educational, and disciplinary needs of their children, the major concern of all parents must be to establish and maintain the kind of home environment within which their growing children can acquire not only initial learning experience in healthy interpersonal relations but also a balanced conception of the meaning of mature personhood as defined in contemporary society. This latter parental goal obviously requires instruction, knowledge, guidance, and encouragement, but most of the values, attitudes, and aims the child internalizes and consequently retains are the result of imitating and identifying with parents as loved and respected models. The family is a major transmission belt of essential values in all societies primarily because parents have incorporated these values in their own way of life and serve as adult models of them to their children.

Applied to Catholic parents who are divorced, this suggests two considerations. In the first place, divorced Catholic parents, like all divorced parents, must recognize that while divorce may modify parent-child relationships, it does not dissolve them. The parents remain significant persons to their children. What they are as adult masculine and feminine persons retains its formative importance. This means that divorced persons who are serious about being parents must first come to terms with each other as individuals, as ex-partners, and as parents of the same children.[13] The actual experience of marital breakdown, formal dissolution and reconstruction is bound to undermine one's sense of security and self-assurance, raise questions regarding loyalty, trust and total commitment, and leave emotional residues of bitterness, guilt, and resentment. Such initial reactions are normal for all but the superficial. They should be admitted, faced honestly, and patiently worked through by each individual. Attempts to deny, suppress, or rationalize such feelings serve only to increase their destructive force. They must be faced, perhaps time and again, and eventually resolved; or better, dissolved through active concern with the real business of living.

Divorced parents are frequently warned that they must

not use their children as pawns in the meaningless game they are tempted to continue to play with each other. Yet this warning will mean very little to parents who are unwilling to face up to their own feelings, for over-concern with themselves and their unsolved personal problems leads them to ignore or misunderstand the real needs of their children. Thus, among other reactions, their unresolved sense of personal failure may lead them to over-protect their children, or they may over-indulge them in compensation for their personal sense of loss. Their unadmitted desire for self-justification may make them so over-anxious about retaining the loyalty of their children that they exaggerate the competitive significance of visiting privileges and overlook the children's need to retain some type of relationship with both parents. More important, they remain incapable of serving as mature adult models, a challenge difficult at best in one-parent families.[14]

In the second place, Catholic parents who are divorced face a number of difficulties in restructuring their lives and serving as models to their children that are not shared by other divorced persons. For example, one of the main elements in Catholic beliefs about marriage is that a valid, consummated marriage between baptized persons is indissoluble. Even the poorly instructed Catholic is well informed on this item of belief, for it is rather generally recognized as one of the major distinguishing marks of the church's teaching on marriage. At least, until recently, Catholics have placed a great deal of emphasis on making a success of their marriages, or, at a minimum, of staying married, for the only legitimate alternative is separation without remarriage. As a result, divorced Catholics normally encounter more disapproval from their relatives and religious community, and experience a greater sense of failure and guilt. These negative reactions are not likely to make the task of personal readjustment after divorce any easier and may lead to some increase of bitterness or resentment at the lack of support and encouragement they receive from those who should best be prepared to understand the special problems they face.[15]

The belief that divorced Catholics should not remarry further increases the difficulties they encounter in restructuring their lives. Our contemporary small family system cannot easily reabsorb its divorced family members or provide for their social fulfillment through appropriate relationships within the extended family circle. This means that the divorced must find other ways of fulfilling their social needs, yet at the same time they must avoid relationships that might lead to serious emotional involvement and remarriage. Many find this too difficult a course to follow and either avoid all extrafamilial social relationships or eventually remarry.

But whether they remarry or remain separated, divorced Catholic parents face added difficulties in explaining divorce to their children. If they remain separated, they must provide not only a model of balanced mature personhood but a Christian conception of conjugal love. This becomes wholly impossible unless both partners show their children that they are loved by both their parents, and both try to help the children to regard their divorce in a non-judgmental manner. This situation is not ideal, of course, but if children are not forced to choose between their parents and are not exposed to open displays of antagonism between them, they are likely to suffer little psychological damage.

If one or both partners remarry, they are automatically excluded from active participation in the sacramental life of the church according to canon law. Catholic parents face a difficult problem here, particularly if they are active church members and their children are old enough to be receiving formal religious instruction. Some explanation should be given when and if the question is raised. As a rule, younger children are satisfied with the assurance that their parents are all right or as good as the parents of others, and that there are personal or technical reasons why they do not frequent the sacraments. Older children are capable of understanding a more adequate explanation, to the effect that life may frequently create situations that do not fit perfectly under the general rule. Under such conditions, one must do the best one can in terms of loving God and neighbor. The general rule still stands as a basic directive for our lives, though exceptional cases must be judged on their own merits.

In discussing the church's marriage doctrine and, specifically, its position regarding the indissolubility of the marriage bond and consequent prohibition on remarriage, I have presented the church's teaching as currently explained and legally defined in canon law. Recently the church's traditional teaching and practice in this regard have been subjected to considerable criticism from canon lawyers, theologians, and others.[16] Some feel that the entire juridical procedure of the church's marriage courts must be thoroughly revised, while others state that its doctrinal presuppositions regarding indissolubility must be carefully reappraised. The code of canon law is currently in the process of being revised, but it is not clear what changes may be made. At any rate, revision will take several years, and in the meantime Catholic marriages will be regulated by the present code.

CONCLUSION

By way of summary I would like to point out that the formal dissolution of a family inevitably gives rise to a number of human problems for which there are no facile solutions. The nature of these problems is shaped to a considerable extent by the marriage beliefs and practices of the couple and the community in which they live. For the most part, the American people have quite ambivalent feelings about divorce. They want it to be easily available, yet don't approve of it. Although divorce is prevalent, it is not yet fully institutionalized. As a result, there exists no clearly defined social norms prescribing how people should treat divorced persons or how divorced persons should behave. Add to this the retention of an outmoded legal superstructure, together with a system of judicial procedures that invite collusion, and one has a fair picture of the current confused state of affairs.

Explaining divorce to children in this social context means helping them come to terms with the practical consequences of their family's dissolution as they personally experience them. One of the major contributions of parents is to present a balanced view of mature personhood and conjugal love. Catholic parents face some special problems in this regard, for they must explain the apparent contradiction between their divorced status and the church's teaching. Since all parents teach primarily by what they are and do rather than by what they say, it seems clear that the first task divorced parents face is to come to terms with their own feelings about themselves and their former partners.

Unfortunately, they receive little help from a society that is unclear about their social status or a church that regards them as a kind of anomaly. When families are dissolved, there are no easy solutions, to be sure. Yet marriages do fail, divorces are granted, and human problems must be faced. Although we may disapprove of, or feel uneasy about divorce in theory, in practice we must work for appropriate, long overdue legal reforms, better marriage preparation, and more adequate counseling facilities for all troubled families.

The strongest formative Jewish influence, continuous and permeating, has been that of the home. Through family life, one serves God. "Man cannot exist without woman, nor woman without man, and both of them without the Lord." Ideally, every human being should live as a unit within a family, for the family is the ideal human group.

Yet, divorce is acceptable in Judaism. To force spouses to live together when the union has lost its sanction and its sanctity is not in the best interests of the family or society. Divorce is not a punishment for a crime but the frank realization that love and mutual respect, the marks of God's presence in a home, are sorely missing.

At the same time, Judaism gives important insights into the relationship of children to families in times of crisis. There is an abundance of sharing religious resources in the encounter with guilt, loneliness, and separation.

Rabbi Earl A. Grollman, D.D., has been the spiritual leader of the Beth El Temple Center in Belmont, Massachusetts since 1951. He has served as Chairman of the Ecumenical Council on Health and Morality and as President of the Massachusetts Board of Rabbis, the only rabbinical group in Massachusetts that serves the needs of Orthodox, Conservative, and Reform Jews.

A RABBI'S VIEWS ON CHILDREN OF DIVORCE

BY *Earl A. Grollman*

LOVE

IN A CHAPTER devoted to Judaism's approach to divorce and children, it is appropriate that we understand a most important word, *Love*. It is perhaps the most abused and overused term in our vocabulary. Love has been exploited by the hucksters for the purpose of selling soap, cosmetics, lingerie, jewelry, and mouthwash. For those contemplating divorce or attempting to teach their children about the meaning of love so that they may someday find marital happiness, Judaism offers insights into the most creative force in human life.

Love is not an ephemeral emotion based upon prosperity or affluence. Love can neither be bought nor sold, the only price being love. Only love satisfies man's need to unite with the world and at the same time to acquire a sense of integrity and individuality. In the act of loving, I am one with all, and yet I am myself. I transcend my personal interest to the interest of the other, but at the same time appreciate the right of differences of opinion. Love does not come about as so many "don'ts," but is the normal fruit of constant cooperation and understanding. Infatuation and sexual needs say: "I love you because I need you." True love counters: "I need you because I love you."

It is two people, standing side by side, facing the world together, seeing approximately the same things, wanting to follow about the same course of action as a consequence. Mature love is an acceptance, an understanding, a tenderness. It does not struggle, or grab, or possess. It sees the other person not as a god or idol, but as a human being possessing the foibles as well as virtues of human beings. It is quiet, gentle, trusting; it is composed of mutual affection and desire.

Love recognizes not only the other's uniqueness (his *haecceitas*) but also what he can become (his *entelechy*). Love, a step in the unfoldment of *homo religiosus,* is man's capacity to live beyond himself in perfect union with another, so that the *I* encompasses the partner in mutual life in an ever-expanding circumference of self-investment. "In love is found the secret of divine unity"; (*Zohar: Exodus*) and in the words of Martin Buber: "He who loves brings God and the World together."

This is Judaism's concept of love. It is more than sexual desire. It is more than an immature and transitory infatuation. Love is a commitment to the true core of its spiritual dimension, a realization of the other's singularity, and the actualizing of his potentiality. It is an old story, yet remains ever new. Love can hope where reason would despair. It is the life of the soul, the harmony of the universe, the master key that opens every heart of man. It is the emblem of eternity, confounding all notions of time, effacing all memory of a beginning, all fear of an end.

When God formed the rose, He said: "Thou shalt flourish and spread thy perfume." When He commanded the sun to emerge from chaos, He added: "Thou shalt give light and warmth to the world." When He created man and woman, He told them to love and said: "If you neglect your love for the other, then in vain do you profess your love for Me."

MARRIAGE

In the book of Genesis (24:67): "And Isaac brought Rebecca into his mother's tent and took Rebecca and she became his wife and he loved her." The late Rabbi Samson Raphael Hirsch suggested that the sequence of verbs is rather unusual. Normally, we would expect the order to be just the reverse—first there is love and then there is marriage that follows. But no, the passage reads that first Isaac took Rebecca to be his wife and then he loved her. The arrangement is correct and deliberate! No matter how important it is that love should precede marriage, it is equally important that it should develop and mature after marriage.

Certainly, it is love that brings a man and woman to the sacred marriage altar; but it is love that continues to keep their marriage altar sacred.

Marriage is an experience in learning to love someone else. In Judaism, it involves husband and wife and God. The marriage relation is referred to in Proverbs (2:17) as a Divine Covenant. The very beginning of the Biblical word declares that "it is not good that man should be alone." (Genesis 2:18) The Judaic viewpoint encourages the love of man and woman not only as a high human fulfillment but as a pathway to the understanding of how profoundly God loves His children. Tradition pictures the very first marriage, that of Adam and Eve, as celebrated with ten magnificent wedding canopies studded with jewels. The angels danced and beat the timbrels while God Himself gave away the bride. The Lord then pronounced the benediction. But why, asked a Roman matron, did God put Adam to sleep when He created Eve? With all His powers, surely He could have taken the rib painlessly even while Adam was awake. The answer: so that Adam should be surprised and delighted when he awoke as he beheld the mystery and the loveliness of his mate.

In Judaism, marriage is regarded as a Divine institution under whose shadow alone there can be true reverence for the mystery, dignity, and sacredness of life. It is a primary religious duty ordained and blessed by God. "Man cannot exist without woman nor woman without man, nor both of them without God." (*Eben Haezar,* 25)

Unlike the ancient Greeks, the Jews regarded the wife with respect and reverence. The non-Jewish scholar, Dr. George Foot Moore, Professor of the History of Religion, Harvard University, asserted that "the woman's legal status under Jewish law compares to its advantage with that of contemporary civilizations." "One who loves his wife as himself and honors her more than himself . . . concerning him does Scripture say, 'And thou shalt know that there is peace in thy tent!' " (*Yebamoth,* 62b) "Man must not cause his wife to weep, for God counts her tears." (*Baba Matzia,* 59a) Equal rights to her children's respect was already initiated in the Ten Commandments: "Honor thy father and thy mother." (Exodus 20:12)

The first of the 613 Biblical commandments is, "Be fruitful and multiply." (Genesis 1:28) Marriage from a Judaic viewpoint has as one of its primary purposes the building of a home. More than in any other nation the family occupies the first and central place in Judaism. Children are indeed what the Psalmist (127:3) calls "a heritage of the Lord." The rabbis declare that among the first questions asked of a person on the day of judgment are, "Did you marry?" and, "Have you founded a family?"

While one of the aims of marriage is procreation, important concomitances are companionship and sexual gratification. When God said, "It is not good for man to be alone," (Genesis 2:18) He was indicating that His plan for husband and wife was not only for the propagation of the race, but also for their mutual welfare and satisfactions. Woman may be a child-bearer but she is also a sex partner. The sexual love relationship is a high adventure of the human spirit, an opportunity for husband and wife to make a oneness of their separateness. One shall not thwart his body, but, rather, sanctify it through love. Voluntary abstinence from sexual relations in marriage is a triple sin— against the health of the body, the fulfillment of the soul, and the welfare of society.

The word used to define marriage in Hebrew is *Kiddushin,* "holiness" which conveys this idea of consecration in the ethical and religious sense. *Wholeness* and *holiness* are inextricably interwoven. Another word is *Nisuin,* "elevation." Marriage is the opportunity to add a new dimension of holiness and to elevate his and her life to one of an infinitely greater happiness and spiritual joy. At the Jewish wedding service, the bride and groom bind themselves to their beloved: "Be thou consecrated (from *Kodesh,* "holy") unto me in accordance with the laws of Moses and Israel." The Jewish home is regarded as the *Mikdash Me'at,* the "miniature sanctuary," where husband and wife are priest and priestess. The words associated with family life are *Shalom bayis,* "peace in the home," which suggest the art of living together in family compatibility. *Horim,* meaning "parents," comes from the same root as *moreh,* "teachers." Parents are the first and foremost teachers. They are to make of their home a germinal cell from which may come forth the spiritual and ethical values of *holiness* and *elevation* of life.

The reciprocal relationship between marriage and religion is clearly seen in Judaism. The important religious rituals are mostly home-centered. Jewish family ceremonials are marked not only by extended family visiting, but by the use of distinctly Jewish foods associated with that particular holy day. Religious observance requires the recitation of blessings at mealtime and at frequent intervals throughout the day. Festivals such as Passover involve extensive participation by family groups in their homes. Some psychiatrists have noted that Jews, more than members of any other group, have reported experiencing their highest religious feelings in a family setting. Yet, the regular celebration of these holidays does not mean that Jewish ritual practices have remained unchanged. On the contrary, since the first three decades of this century there has been a marked alteration or abbreviation of home ritual ceremonies on the part of most American Jewish families. However, it is not the extent of these ceremonies which is of concern but their *function* as a binding influence on the family.

Within the Jewish family setting, customs, associations, and values have helped the family withstand many of the disruptive influences of modern life. By preserving these practices, the Jewish family has, in effect, preserved itself against some of the disorganization that is currently widespread in American family life.

Love and marriage in crisis

Mark Twain once said: "The Jewish home is a home in the truest sense." Sociologists have often accentuated the solidarity of the Jewish family as the prime reason for the small percentage of criminality, alcoholism, juvenile delinquency, sexual promiscuity, and divorce attributed to them. Yet, in America today, the evolving customs of a complicated society are bringing on—with increasing seriousness—a disruptive change. It is revealed in the shifting, puzzling relationship between husband and wife, the courting habits of young people, and the staggering increase in family disorganization.

For Jewish people, the question is now asked: Can Jewish values enrich the mainstream without being swamped in the churning tides of the general milieu? A Chassidic rabbi once explained that there were two major tragedies which could befall the Jews. One was to be stripped of their liberty and forced to live in ghettos. When this happened in the past, the Torah flourished even as the spiritual values were cherished, yet the restrictions that were imposed were too great a burden to bear. The other tragedy, the rabbi asserted, would be for Jews to live free and unrestricted among their countrymen, but with the Torah forgotten and things of the spirit lost.

In the United States today, anti-Semitism is at an all-time low and publicly out of fashion. Jews are experiencing an unprecedented freedom never known in ancient Israel or the golden age in Moslem Spain. There is freedom to adhere to the faith or abandon it; to emphasize differences or to do away with them entirely. For the time being, the Jew has gained a sense of security in a new history without tears. He has progressed economically at an even more rapid pace than the country as a whole. In education he is at a par with the more culturally advanced segments of the American population.

He is part of the Great Divide in American Jewish history. His generation has achieved full acculturation in the acquired values of the United States. Unlike his immigrant parents or grandparents, he is American born, American educated, and an inherent part of the American middleclass. Since the end of World War II, the greatest change affecting the interactions of American Jewry with other Americans has been the rapid and far-reaching population shift from the cities to the suburbs. Two-thirds of American Jews live in suburban sections of major metropolitan areas, often next door to Christian neighbors. For two thousand years the Jews have learned to "sing the Lord's song" in bondage; now it remains to be seen whether they will learn how to sing His song in freedom.

Many have tried to eliminate and suppress those differences which distinguish them from other American groups. As the Jew strives to achieve "Americanization," he has a tendency to be more "like" other Americans and less "unlike." When he was denied equality, he fought fiercely to be different. Now that he is regarded as an equal, he tends to accept mediocrity posing as normalcy. Jewish group distinctiveness pales in proportion. The bonds between the Jew and his family life are loosed. The scales of values are leveled off. The assimilatory process aids in breaking down those social controls which were once inherent in the social pattern of this tightly knit and relatively isolated group.

The sense of disintegration in Jewish life is related to the general crisis of values in American life. Rabbis are asked, how to achieve a distinctive religio-cultural identity that stresses Jewish family values and at the same time participate fully in an integrated and pluralist America. Can the rivulet of Jewish distinctiveness maintain itself against the onrushing sea of mass American mores?

It is difficult to ascertain the degree of family discord of respective religious groups in the United States. The agencies which collect data on marriage and divorce do not use such classifications. Nor does the Bureau of Census report the status of the population according to ethnic origin. Yet it would be accurate to maintain that there is today a loss of Jewish family values. Dramatic weakening ties in family life, the widening gulf in parent-child relationships, the rising divorce rate within the Jewish community provide significant warning signals that the home-centered tradition of the heritage is fast becoming the most tragic casualty in the new generation of American Jewry. For Jews and for all Americans, the impact of a country in crisis is profound, shocking, and disorganizing. Old standards are being constantly challenged and discarded; new ones are not yet established. The Jewish family unit is fragmented. Louis Z. Grant, a Chicago Jewish attorney who specializes in matrimonial law, has asserted that there has been a tenfold increase in divorces among Jews during the preceding decade. Many rabbis agree, and give documented proof of the growing number of divorces in their own congregations. The price of the family disunity is found not just in the statistics of sociologists but in the hearts of children and separated parents.

DIVORCE

All marriages, like all lives, must end. Some end by death and some by divorce. Some exist for years as a mere formality.

Judaism believes in the holiness of marriage but will not preserve the legal family at *all* costs. Mosaic law does not subscribe to the view that "what therefore God hath joined together, let no man put asunder" and that "the wife departeth not from her husband." Divorce may be a tragedy; but if the marriage was ill-advised in the first place, it may be an inevitable one.

As a Jewish institution, divorce had its origin in pre-Israelitic times. The Torah states: "When a man taketh a wife and marrieth her, then it cometh to pass if she finds no favor in his eyes, because he hath found some unseemly thing in her, that he writeth her a bill of divorce and giveth it in her hand, and sendeth her out of his house." (Deuteronomy 24:1)

The basis of this Jewish law is the absolute authority of the husband. The house belonged to him. The wife was under his rule. In the legal systems of the ancient near Eastern peoples, the right to divorce was always accorded the male spouse. If he for any reason became dissatisfied, he could send his wife away from his house, thereby dissolving the marital bond. He might simply pronounce an oral formula: "Because she is not my wife, and I am not her husband." (Hosea 2:4)

In the course of time, the unrestricted rights of the husband have been tempered by numerous limiting measures. Malachi (about 445 B.C.E.) declared that marriage was sacred, and appealed to the honorable conscience of the husband. Even though marriage was a contract between husband and wife, he said that God is the ever-present witness. He castigated those who deal treacherously against the "wife of thy covenant." (2:14–16) The prophet acknowledges that divorce is permitted by the Torah, but it is hateful to God. Yet separation can take place because people are human. When marriages die, divorce becomes a calamitous necessity.

In the first century, there was a dispute over the text of Deuteronomy (22:13–28) on grounds for divorce. Shammai held that a man could not lawfully divorce his wife except for immoral acts such as unchastity or adultery. (This sounds like some of the laws in our country.) Hillel, the leader of the other rabbinical school of thought, took a different approach. His interpretation was that a man could dissolve the marriage if he found anything "offensive" in her, even if she had "merely spoilt his food." The opinion of the school of Hillel prevailed. Grounds were not required for his dissolution of the marriage.

While not completely overruled, the ancient theory of the husband's unrestricted privilege of divorce was moderated by the Mishnah (the collection of *halachoth* or laws by Judah Hanasi and his colleagues, about 200 C.E.). New restraints were added to the other two grounds in the Torah: the husband "shall not be at liberty to put her away all his days" if he had ravished her before marriage, (Deuteronomy 22:28–29) or if he had falsely accused her of unchastity during betrothal. (Deuteronomy 22:13–21) The husband could not divorce his wife if she were insane, or in captivity, or a minor and too young to understand the procedures of the bill of divorcement. The Mishnah further modified the absolute right of the husband to the dissolution of the marriage by making the legal entanglements more difficult.

Other curbs were placed on the husband's theoretical

right to divorce his wife. The *Kethubah* (marriage contract) contained the obligation of the husband to pay a certain sum to his wife in the event of divorce. The Talmudic teachers, in the third to fifth centuries C.E., were zealous in insuring that the wife would receive all her rights as provided in the document; namely, that the husband would return all of the property that she had brought into the marriage as well as any other amount he may have assigned as her marriage portion. Another stipulation required that a divorce take place in the presence of a court of rabbis (*Beth Din,* "tribunal"), offering her still more safeguards as well as, for both of them, possibilities of reconciliation. Finally, in the eleventh century, by a decree of Rabbi Gershom of Mayence, the complete authority of the husband to divorce his wife came to a formal end. This famous decree states (*Responsa Asheri,* 42:1): "To assimilate the right of the woman to the right of the man, it is decreed that even as the man does not put away his wife except of his own free will, so shall the woman not be put away except by her own consent. Where either of the parties shows good cause for divorce, the marriage will be dissolved against the will of the guilty party" (*Eben Haezar,* 119:6). Moses Maimonides (1135–1204) stated that, "If a woman says 'My husband is distasteful to me; I cannot live with him,' the court compels the husband to divorce her, because a wife is not a captive." (*Yad: Ishut,* 14:8)

The wife's right to sue for divorce—unknown in the Biblical law—was now radically altered. In traditional Judaism today, a wife has grounds for divorce if her husband is impotent; if he has since marriage contracted some loathsome disease like leprosy; if he, after marriage, engages in an occupation that makes him so physically disgusting as to make cohabitation impossible; if he refuses to support her; if he is guilty of cruel and abusive treatment; if he changes his Jewish religion; if he is guilty of wife-beating; or if he commits an offense that causes him to flee the country.

A husband can obtain a divorce if his wife is guilty of adultery; if she obstinately refuses for one year to allow the husband the exercise of his conjugal rights; if there is public flaunting of the code of moral decency and feminine modesty; if she is lax in religious observances or has left the Jewish faith; if she has contracted an incurable disease which makes intercourse impossible or dangerous; if she is incapable of bearing children; if the marriage remains childless after ten years; or if she refuses to move to her husband's place of domicile.

In Jewish law, there is nothing reprehensible in divorce by consent of wife and husband. By mutual agreement of both parties, the Rabbinical Court will grant their request for divorce. It is not required to investigate further or to condemn either spouse as the "offender." The tribunal is only concerned that both parties are acting in complete understanding, without deception or duress, so that no suspicion be cast upon the legality and validity of the divorce.

Financial support stipulated in the *Kethubah* is forthcoming to the woman as a monetary settlement. According to Jewish law, the court does not grant a divorce or issue a decree. Husband and wife divorce each other, with the former granting the divorce to the latter.

Thus, Judaism still affirms the concept of marriage as holiness, *Kiddushin*. However, when the basic ingredients of love, communication, respect, and emotional support are missing, the Judaic viewpoint is that the holy institution of marriage is terminable. There is no suggestion that husband and wife must remain together "for the sake of the children." One does not maintain the values of marriage by preserving the empty form.

Procedures in obtaining a Jewish divorce

Ceremonials play an important part in Jewish life. Each significant crisis situation is invested with religious significance. At birth, there is circumcision for the boy and special prayers in the synagogue for girls. Puberty is the time of Bar and Bas Mitzvah, in which Torah (learning) is the keynote. Marriage has the stamp of Divinity—the oneness and holiness of man and woman—in family harmony. The traditions surrounding death are structured by definite and solemn procedures.

Divorce is also a time of emotional extremity. The religious ritual of divorce is peculiar to Jews. Spiritual overtones are conferred upon these moments of pain and separation. Since a Jewish man and woman are married not only by the authority of the state but by religious vows as well, a severance is not traditionally completed by the obtaining of a civil divorce alone. There is a formal procedure within Jewish law.

The manner of divorce is described in the book of Deuteronomy: If the husband wishes to send away his wife, he "writeth her a bill of divorcement (*Sefer Kerithuth*) and giveth it in her hand." (24:1) No further embellishments are stated as to the formula employed in the Biblical document. The popular term for divorce is *Get*. The word signifies any formal written instrument such as a bill of sale, but the specialized meaning in post-Talmudic times has been "bill of divorce." The prerequisites for a *Get* are the consent of both partners and the husband's direct authorization before a rabbi for the writing, signing, and transmission of the divorce to his wife. The *Get* is a religious document of twelve lines of text. The number 12 was chosen because that is the numerical value of *Get* in Hebrew: *Gimel* (3) + *Teth* (9) = 12. It bears the signature of two witnesses and attests to the termination of the state of marriage.

The divorce is written in the presence of a rabbinical tribunal of three. Regulations governing the issuing of a *Get* are cited in minute detail. For example, the ink must be clean and black; the pen is to be made from a goosequill; the paper must be in perfect condition without erasures or holes. Every phase of the *Get* is ordered and precise.

As the woman's interests are protected in the Jewish marriage, so are they safeguarded in Jewish divorce. The husband must pay the wife the amount specified in the *Kethubah* and return her dowry. The settlement of the property rights of the couple takes place either at the same time as the divorce or some time previously.

After the proceedings, the document is returned to the rabbi, who makes an incision in it, and keeps it in his permanent file. He then issues to each party an official statement (*P'tur*) signed by the court attesting to the completion of the divorce. Both parties are then free to remarry in accordance with the laws of Moses and Israel. Before leaving the tribunal, both are blessed with the hope that they may someday find happiness and peace.

Orthodox and Conservative rabbis today still require a *Get* before the remarriage of a divorced person, i.e., before the divorce is considered final. (In 1954 the Conservative movement added a paragraph to the marriage contracts requiring that in case of marital difficulty each couple pledge themselves to return to the rabbi who performed the ceremony or his representative.) Reform Jews do not deem a *Get* necessary. They refer back to the historical changes in the nineteenth and twentieth centuries when country after country established their own civil laws of divorce, thus circumscribing the powers of the Jewish court. *Dina d'Malchusa dina*—the law of the land is legal.

Is marriage more than a civil ceremony? A prominent liberal rabbi, Joseph Klein of Temple Emanuel, Worcester,

Massachusetts has written (in a letter to this editor): "My own feeling is that the subject of divorce in Reform Judaism is very much in need of being reopened for discussion. I do not think that our present system in which a civil divorce is regarded as sufficient and binding is completely satisfactory. If we insist upon a religious marriage, there ought also to be a religious form of divorce in addition to the civil require- ments. I feel that it is quite possible for the Central Confer- ence of American Rabbis [Reform] to devise a *Get* which will be issued by a *Beth Din* of three rabbis when a divorce is unavoidable. Provision can also be made for issuing a *Get* to a woman whose husband refuses to involve himself in a religious divorce. While this would not be completely in accordance with Talmudic law, nevertheless, it would indi- cate that we are trying to act in the spirit of the *halachah*. Certainly a divorce that has religious sanction behind it would have psychological values for the people involved which our present system does not offer. But the most im- portant consideration, it seems to me, would be the fact that a rabbi, by his refusal to remarry people who have not obtained a religious divorce, would have opportunities that he does not now possess in attempting to bring about recon- ciliation in homes that are breaking up."

In the past, the formal procedure of the *Get* aided in re- ducing the number of hasty and impetuous divorces. The requirement to give the wife a written document afforded the couple an opportunity to reflect and reconsider their decision. When divorce was effected, the woman's property rights were safeguarded. Also, the husband was protected. With the bill of divorcement, he was no longer responsible for her conduct or debts. Most important, a religious conno- tation was applied to the crisis of separation.

Have conditions altered the usefulness of the *Get*? With

civil divorce, is the dissolution of the marriage now complete? In the words of Rabbi Solomon Freehof, "Are those
who insist upon a *Get* a dwindling minority?" Are not the
economic and legal provisions already established, since the
Get in no way modifies the legal conditions agreed upon in
the civil divorce? What possibility is there for reconciliation
when the man and woman are currently legally divorced?
What happens if the divorced person without a religious
divorce falls in love with someone of the Conservative or
Orthodox denomination and the desired rabbi will not offi-
ciate? Does the *Get* still possess important historical, spiritual,
and psychological values? Has the *Get* lost its significance?
These are questions far easier to ask than to answer.

Custody of children in Jewish divorce

The Jewish sages recognized a basic psychological truth.
In early times, the husband possessed the ancient power of
pater familias. The woman, however, had the religious duty
of rearing her children. There is a popular expression:
"God could not be everywhere, so He created mothers."

The rabbis understood that the mother was irreplaceable.
This is certainly substantiated by the findings of modern
science. We know today that a few hours after birth a baby
begins to feel the sensations of hunger and thirst. To remove
these pains, he must be fed. He finds pleasure in the act of
sucking which helps the rhythm of breathing and digestion.
He needs the nearness of the mother and the security of her
body. Realizing her importance to the child, authorities
granted custody of the infant to the mother, if she so desired.

Early Mishnaic regulations considered the wife's maternal
responsibilities as all-important. "The following are the
kinds of work which a woman must perform for her hus-

band: Grinding corn, baking bread, washing clothes, cooking, suckling her child." (*Kethuboth,* 59b) The mother was responsible for the care and custody of the infant.

After the woman is divorced, she is still the mother. Only she can render to her progeny a unique sense of well-being and emotional satisfaction. There is a story of a divorced lady who told Samuel that she would not nurse her son. Samuel then asked Rabbi Dimi ben Joseph to test her case and determine whether the child knew his mother. "Rabbi Dimi went and placed her among a row of women and, taking hold of her child, carried him in front of them. When he came up to her, the child looked at her face with joy but she turned away from him. 'Lift up your eyes,' he called to her. 'Come, take away your son.' . . . How does a blind child know its mother? Rabbi Ashi said: By the smell and the taste (of the milk)." (*Kethuboth,* 60a) The mother is to the infant the most "significant other."

If the wife requested custody, the husband was obliged to support her children even after she had remarried. For a specific period of time she could retain her offspring against her husband's wishes, because only she could perform the necessary motherly duties. "Our Rabbis taught: A child must be breast fed for 24 months. . . . Rabbi Joshua said: He may be breast fed even for four or five years." (*Kethuboth,* 65b) Rabbi Ulla made the following exposition: "Although it was said, a man is under no obligation to maintain his sons and daughters when they are minors, he must maintain them when they are very, very young. How long must he maintain them? Until the age of six." (*Kethuboth,* 102b)

The mother was to relinquish the sons, but the daughters she could keep indefinitely. The father's role was explicit. "He is bound in respect of his son to circumcise him, redeem him, teach him Torah, take a wife for him, and teach him a craft." (*Kethuboth*, 29a) When the boy was six, he was required to live with the father with whom he would study and learn. Torah was exclusively the province of the world of men. The tradition of separating the son helped him to leave the mother's "apron-strings" and establish a strong identification with his paternal elders.

Today rabbinical courts award the custody of children at their own discretion. (*Eben Haezer*, 8:2:7, note) Once again, we see how Jewish law has been viable in order to meet the needs of its adherents. Man, in search of God, discovers Him only through gradual stages. Jewish life is an evolutionary process of discovery and interpretation. Tribunals are given the widest latitude to act *in the best interests of the youngsters*. The important question is the most religious and humane: Who will contribute most to the children's physical welfare and to their spiritual and emotional security? How best to help children of divorce?

Jewish literary sources guide us in helping children of divorce

Nothing is more disturbing to a child than a change he does not understand. Parents must help their offspring to face reality, just as they too must face it. "Blessed is he in whom is truth." (II Enoch 42:12) "A little truth overcomes much deception, as a little light dispels much darkness." (Bahya, *Hobot HaLabot*, 5:5) "Falsehood begets falsehood." (Levi, *Midrash Tehillim*, 7:11) "A liar's punishment is that he is not believed even when he tells the truth." (*Sanhedrin*, 89b) Be honest with the youngsters about the divorce. It may be painful, but so is an unexplained separation.

Don't make promises that you cannot keep. It is wisely recommended, "A person should never tell a child that he will give him something and not keep his vow because he thereby teaches the child to tell lies." (*Sukkah*, 46b) "The principal cause of misdeeds is familiarity with falsehood" (Philo, *Special Laws,* 4:10). If there is no possibility of reconciliation, do not mislead with distorted hopes. "A word unfulfilled is like thunder without rain." (Hasdai, *Ben HaMelek,* 5)

The former husband and wife should not deprecate each other. They still remain father and mother. Personal grievances must be pushed into the background for the sake of the offspring. "If you know an evil matter, bury it seven fathoms underground." (*Ahikar,* 2:54) "Be not like a fly, seeking sore spots. Cover up your mate's flaws and reveal them not to the children." (Eliezar ben Isaac, *Ornot Hayyim*) "God loves not destroyers of reputation, even when they are right." (Ibn Ezra, *Shirat Yisrael*) "Cruel talk kills three: the speaker, the spoken of, and the listener." (*Numbers Rabbah,* 19:2) Don't malign and disparage the other partner!

Children should never have the guilty feeling that they are to blame for their parents' tensions. "Fear builds a wall to bar the light." (Baal Shem, *Tales of the Hasidim,* 1:42) Often, parents will say to their youngsters: "If it weren't for you, I would not have to worry about so many things." The children, therefore, feel they are responsible for the unrest and unhappiness. A Judaic dictum admonishes adults to be very cautious in what they say to the young: "The talk of the child in the streets is that of his father and mother." (*Sukkah,* 56b)

Don't take out your aggressions on your offspring. "One should not terrorize his children." (*Gittin,* 6b) When you are vexed with their ways, remember the days of your own youth. On the other hand, the children should not be overindulged in order to compensate for your own failures. "If one refrains from punishing a child, he will end by becoming utterly depraved." (*Exodus Rabbah,* 1:1) The Talmud-

ists blame the corrupt character of Absalom (who led a
revolt against his father, King David) upon his pampered
youth. The proper course is balance: "To push away with
the left hand and draw them near with the right hand."
(*Semochoth,* 2:6)

One should not try to impose impossible standards on
children. No matter how the subject of divorce is presented,
the youngsters' lives are changed. Even if the family were
to remain together in peace and harmony, *all* children have
difficulties in growing up. If you set their goals too high,
both you and they will be hurt. "Perfection belongs only to
God." (Ibn Ezra, *Shirat Yisrael,* 71) Nor should you bring
unhappiness by your insistence that the children make up
for your failures. Some parents deny it, but they are frequently looking for victories and satisfactions for themselves
rather than for their offspring.

Listen to what your children are saying. Many parents
are so intent on explaining their "side" of the divorce that
they do not take time to hear and heed what their offspring
have to say. "Man was endowed with two ears and one
tongue, that he may listen more than speak." (Hasdai, *Ben
HaMelek,* 26) "Hearken and you will learn." (Ibn Gabirol,
Midbar HaPeninim, 19) "When people hear each other, the
Holy One listens to them too; and if they do not, they cause
the Divine Presence to depart." (Simon b. LaKish, *Sab-
bath,* 63a)

Children should be able to express their feelings, even
those of fear, anguish, and hostility. "Emotions become
more violent when expression is stifled." (Philo, *Joseph,* 2)
"Since the destruction of the Temple, all gates of prayer
have been closed except to the cry of hurt feelings." (Hisda,
Baba Metzia, 59a) The late Joshua Loth Liebman used to
say: "Thou shalt not be afraid of thy hidden impulses."

To empathize is to reverse your role and to imagine how

the children might feel during this time of crisis. "Only feeling understands feeling." (*Orhot Tzaddikim*, 15c) "A parent without sensibility is less than an ant." (*Leviticus Rabbah*, 1:15)

Be patient. Don't expect miracles overnight. The children are probably doing their best to make painful adjustments. But it takes time and forbearance. The ability to wait and not overwhelm requires courage and strength. "Patience yields many good things." (*Patriarchs, Joseph*, 2:7) "Through perseverance, one can avert still greater trouble. Misfortune may become fortune through unhurried actions." (Ibn Gabirol, *Midbar HaPeninim*, 104, 146) For patience is the preserver of peace and the teacher of perspective. Time is sometimes the wisest counselor.

The young need praise as well as older people. At a time of crisis, children need to know that they are wanted and needed. When they are deserving of commendation, your on-the-spot recognition will do much to demonstrate that they are appreciated. Yet there is something sweeter than receiving praise—the feeling of having merited it. From truly earned praise, the children will experience justifiable self-worth and esteem. "Praise is comely for the righteous." (Psalms 33:1) Approval may be one of the most important ingredients in affording the children encouragement and reassurance.

Each child's response to divorce will be different. A Chassidic rabbi said it this way: "Each person experiences distress in accordance with the stature of his soul and the tolerance of his body." Just as no two blades of grass are exactly alike, so no children are precisely the same, even identical twins. The sages drove home this point in a vivid parable. "A mortal king," they said, "when he wishes to make many coins, creates one mold. With that form, he stamps out all the coins he needs. Each coin is exactly like every other coin. God, however, created all men from one. Yet no two individuals are exactly alike." So each youngster is unique in himself and his own life situation. No one in the world duplicates him. That which is relevant is only that which is meaningful to a particular child at a given moment. Help him to discover and develop his own uniqueness.

God said to David: "If life is what you seek, meditate on suffering, for the reproofs of instruction are the ways of life." (*Yalkut,* Psalm 67) Of course children are pained by the separation. But life itself cannot be described without the element of hurt. What gives light must endure burning. Children might be bitter at first, but they must learn to face adversity. Pangs belong to life and cannot be eliminated either through flight or fancy. Sweetness alone is impossible for a complete existence. Darkness and light, joy and sorrow, success and suffering—all of these are indispensable strands. Neither parents nor children seek a crisis, but when it comes they must make the best of it, not in surrender but in constructive action. "As the olive does not give of its precious oil except under pressure, so Israel does not bring forth its highest virtues except through adversity." (*Exodus Rabbah*) In many a sigh is found an insight. There is no predicament that we and our offspring cannot ennoble either by doing or enduring. Divorce can be transmuted into an instrument to enhance a child's spiritual nature by enlarged sympathy, courageous acceptance, and active determination; that is, to reshape hardship into hardihood, misery into mercy, and to strive for that keener insight that finally allowed Job to cry out even in travail: "I know that my Redeemer liveth. . . . In mine own time will I see God." (19:25)

The most important help in your children's suffering is your love. The power to love is a privilege which God has given us, and not a pistol with which to hold up and control others' destinies. In the story of the Akedah (Genesis 22), Abraham was in danger of loving God so much that he would have destroyed his own son, Isaac. The ancient patriarch finally understood that Isaac needed his love more than God wanted it. Your children need your love. There is no more critical moment when your offspring require parental affection than during the crisis of divorce. They have every right to fear the future. Their home is split and they feel abandoned. Let them know that they are wanted and needed even though husband and wife no longer live together. For there is one facet of your marriage both of you need never relinquish—you can always be your children's loving parents. Banish fear and anxiety from their gates by inviting love and security within their portals.

Your goal now is to return to the task, renew your efforts, and restore your strength. There is the story of a student who sat before the *Zaddik,* "the righteous," Rabbi Mordecai of Nadvorna. Shortly before the Jewish New Year the young man asked for permission to be dismissed. The Rabbi asked: "Why are you hurrying?" The answer: "I am a reader in the synagogue, and I must look into the prayer book and put my prayers in order." The *Zaddik* replied: "The prayer book is the same as it was last year. It would be better for you to look into your own deeds and put yourself in order."

How to help your children during the crisis of divorce? A great deal will depend on how you have first put yourself in order. May you use your lips for truth, your voice for prayer, your eyes for pity, your hands for charity, your heart for abiding love.

REMARRIAGE

Once the couple is divorced, Jewish law looks with favor upon their respective remarriages. (*Eduyot,* 4:7) "As long as there is life, there is hope." (*Berakot*, 9:1) It is true that the present marriage has failed, but to be a Jew is to be an optimist. Tomorrow may be better. Where there is no confidence, there can be no endeavor. The Mosaic faith challenges: "Go on! Go on!" Hope is like the wings of an angel, soaring up to heaven and bearing prayers to the throne of God. Extinguish it and the gloom of affliction becomes the very blackness of darkness—cheerless and impenetrable.

Remarriage is another chance for happiness if you have truly learned from the past and can profit from your experiences. You acquire wisdom from failure as well as success. A rabbi once said that he became better acquainted with a country because he had the good fortune to frequently lose his way and discover the exciting and less frequented back roads and landscapes.

The theme of Jewish law is: "Thou shalt not make unto thee any false images of thyself." So you made a mistake. "All flesh doth frailty breed." But wallowing in self-pity is not the answer. Nor is it good for the children. Just remember that anyone can make an error, but none but a fool will continue in it.

THE SYNAGOGUE AND RABBI

The rabbi is the one who joins two lives into one, calls for the exchange of faithful vows, and blesses the union "in accordance with the faith of Moses and of Israel." His responsibility should not end at the altar, any more than the couple's. If they remain in his community and attend his synagogue, he should have a continuing relationship with them, standing by them in every crisis, and giving them and their offspring the faithful attention of genuine interest and concern.

As one who cares deeply about family life, it is his responsibility to become better informed about his all-important role in premarital and marital counseling. Yet, the rabbi is not omniscient. He may be of service only if he is *aware* of disharmony in the home. It is too late to see him when love has fled and the break has become final.

The noted psychiatrist Dr. Nathan W. Ackerman pointed out that "in our clinical work, we are impressed with the fact that people do not marry well from the beginning." In the premarital interviews, the rabbi should not only be concerned with the rituals of the ceremony. He should also deal with the depth meaning of personality and emotional conflicts that could hinder the two lives being merged into a sacred unity. Proverbially, marriages may be made in heaven. However, they must be lived here on earth. How will the couple face questions of financial responsibility, sex, in-law problems? In his interview, the rabbi is afforded the opportunity (unlike the marriage counselor and psychologist) of fostering mutual trust and a shared interest in spiritual and religious activities. He stresses the importance of such things as compatibility, mutual affection, children, and family life, not as an expedient ethic but as a categorical imperative of Jewish life.

The spirit that represents premarital guidance is one of anticipation. In marital crisis counseling, the atmosphere is characterized by the emotional problem of estrangement. There are no cut and dried answers to the recondite problems that are posed. But the rabbi can initially assist by demonstrating an unshakable attitude of acceptance towards the troubled people. Much depends on this quality. It should be not only one of words but a non-verbal communication of empathy; not the moment of pontifical moralizing, but of loving support and understanding. The rabbi is most effective when he acts like a rabbi—not an amateur psychiatrist. As a religious leader of the Jewish community, he extends his loving concern in imparting a religious orientation of life, a power of faith, and a meaningful belief in the God of life.

If the couple decide after counseling that they will sever their relationship, the rabbi must not take it as a personal affront. It is their lives at stake and the future of their progeny, not the vanity of the spiritual leader. What purpose is being served in their continuing to torture each other (and indirectly their offspring) for the rest of their lives? Divorce is never a complete solution. The wounds that ensue are deep. But divorce may be a necessary step to a solution.

When all efforts towards understanding and reconciliation have failed, the rabbi may be of inestimable value in helping the couple through their separation and divorce. He, or by his referral a therapist, may assist the couple to gain insight into what went wrong with the marriage. He can aid in the ensuing personal crises such as guilt, frustration, purposelessness, feelings of inferiority, and intense discouragement. Acting in a symbolic role for the God of forgiveness, he may greatly assist in relieving the feelings of the troubled and tormented souls. God forgives, and so must His children. We are to learn from the past and then transform the errors of yesterday into stepping stones leading onward and upward for tomorrow.

Children of divorce also need help during these difficult times. They may want to spill out their feelings of anxiety and resentment. To whom can they turn? To their peer groups? No, they are too abashed to even talk to their friends about those events that could evoke so much shame and dishonor. The parents? So often, they are too engrossed in their own emotional entanglements. But the rabbi is friend and leader. He can be spoken to without threat of reprisal. He might also suggest a temple youth group where the youngster could break away from the tense home en-

vironment and join with others of his own age in exciting
interests and activities.

For *all* children, prevention is better than cure. Our
young people should be better informed about Jewish views
of love, sex, and the family. If Judaism is a way of life, then
preparation for marriage must become part and parcel of
religious school instruction. A realistic program of life
education begins when youngsters first begin to ask those
"embarrassing" questions; they should not be deferred to the
post-confirmation class. Multi-disciplinary experts such as
psychologists, educators, social workers, marriage counselors, and physicians should be asked to participate in these
joint efforts. Representatives of Jewish Family and Children's Service are wonderful resource personnel. A course
in community agencies could prove invaluable in informing
the entire congregation of the help these specialized organizations can render them, should they ever need it. There
is so much that can be done to give our children a better
insight into the problems they may later meet. Mr. Clark W.
Blackburn, General Director of the Family Service Association of America, declared: "We, the family life professionals, the counselors, the teachers, must do a far better job of
training young people for the realities of marriage than we
have been doing. . . . We should . . . attempt to change
the basic institutions and organizational patterns that shape
the lives of people rather than confine ourselves to problem-
solving."

And some of our "organizational patterns" are woefully
weak. Synagogues might work together in urging a revision
of many of our antiquated, unjust, and dishonest divorce
laws. Certainly the time has arrived for the enactment of
uniform marriage, divorce, and desertion statutes. We could
galvanize our combined efforts to provide more adequate
facilities for the ending of unworkable marriages in a dig-

nified and sympathetic manner. Our present divorce court procedures are an affront to the dignity of the separating husband and wife and their children. We could strive to bring into our juvenile and domestic relations courts decent auxiliary social services to better diagnose the cases in question and apply all of the necessary professional skills to help the parents and their progeny.

The synagogue can and should do more. Formerly married people are often discriminated against in our institutions. They just do not feel welcome at family gatherings and social affairs where couples are prominent. Their usual comment: "I feel like a fifth wheel." The divorcee, especially, is considered a threat, as someone "on the make," as one who is "fast with men." (Compare this with the widow, whose loss is freely discussed and who is lovingly encouraged after the funeral to return to her temple work.) Rabbi and congregation should have the sensitivity to help *all* who have suffered separation during their difficult period of adjustment and aloneness.

Divorced people should therefore be part and parcel of our religious and communal activities. Their talents could be utilized and made a part of our larger fellowship. In addition, they need to share with like-minded people their feelings, troubles, and hopes. Just as there is a Golden Age Club for the aged, why not an organization for the formerly married? There should be a place where they could join with those in similar positions. One clergyman, Reverend Ronald E. Whittal, organized such a group. He wrote: "To really assess what is being accomplished here you should have known these people when they came to their first meetings. Their faces were drawn, most were nervous and shy. Some just sat and stared and were totally uncommunicative. Now look at them! They're animated. They share their problems and share in the solutions. The change begins when they find their problems aren't unique, that others have faced the same troubles and worked their way out."

Marriages fail: either because they were improperly constituted or because of changes in the personality needs of the couple and their resultant relationship. Frequently, those who are divorced are in need of help. They may be shunned by society for committing a "terrible sin." They may be left without a group in which to participate or even a friend in whom to confide. Their children, too, are frightened and alone. It is the sacred responsibility of the synagogue to aid these people in gaining new insights and experiences that will allow for a more positive conditioning in their relationships with themselves, their faith, and their God.

EPILOGUE

Marriage is *Kiddushin*, "holiness." One completes the other through matrimony. *Kiddushin* is to care, to assume responsibility for, to respect, to cherish the qualities and the promise of the person who is loved and loves in return.

In Judaism, people are more important than institutions. The stability of marriage must, if necessary, be sacrificed to the right of the individual to attain personal fulfillment. Marriage was made for man, and not man for marriage. Rashi, the popular expounder of the Bible and the Talmud, wrote: "If thou hatest her, then put her away; but act not cruelly by retaining her in the home if thou art estranged from her." The futile act of preserving the union at all costs is neither desirable for the couple nor the general welfare of their progeny.

At best, divorce is a difficult and shaking experience. It means the end of family life as the child has known it, the end of feeling that his parents are there whenever he wants them. The youngster may not understand the legal arrangements of divorce, but he very much perceives the loss of a parent. And yet, staying together for the sake of the children may be more destructive. The offspring's happiness may be better served by a divorce than a hate-ridden, quarrel-filled marriage.

How the divorced parents accept their child could well determine how the child accepts himself. Your friendliness helps him to be friendly; your trustworthiness helps him to be trustworthy; and your hostility may cause him to be hostile. See him as a personality to be released, not as a burden to be endured. Impart the significance of reliability and faith not only by the language of words but the language of relationship. Demonstrate that he is truly loved and needed.

Judaism offers you and your children an abundance of religious resources in the encounter with helplessness, guilt, loneliness, and fear. The goal of synagogue and rabbi is the emergence of a new self which has assimilated the grief experience and grown because of and through it.

And, finally, a Hebrew word that is mentioned for the first time in this chapter, *T'shuva*. It means "to return"—the opportunity of a renewal attempt, a fresh start, the ever-new beginning. Your past failures need not doom you forever. The willingness to build the temple of tomorrow's dreams on the graves of yesterday's bitterness and disappointment is the greatest evidence of the Divine unquenchable light that fires the soul of mankind. You and your children are now to march up the dark slopes toward the light that glimmers over the edge of the next rise. With the Psalmist may you yet affirm: "Though weeping tarries in the night, joy cometh with the morning."

CHAPTER X

This book is a compilation of the latest information and perspectives from the fields of psychology, psychiatry, sociology, law, and religion. The experts have spoken.

Now six youngsters whose parents were divorced give their honest reactions in this last chapter: "Would a Broken Home Break You?" which was a lead article in the March 1968 issue of SEVENTEEN *Magazine.*

CHILDREN OF DIVORCE, THEIR PERSONAL VIEWS: "WOULD A BROKEN HOME BREAK YOU?"

MODERATOR: *How did you feel about your parents' divorce?*

STEVE: I wasn't surprised; I was only eleven at the time, but they'd been fighting ever since I could remember. When they went out at night we never knew whether they'd come home together, if at all. The divorce was a relief. Living that way was horrible for me and my brothers and sisters.

ROBIN: I was only two when it happened, so I don't remember how I felt. If I'd been older, I doubt that I'd have been surprised, though, because I could never understand how they came to be married in the first place.

LYNN: My parents were divorced three years ago. I felt it had been coming for a long time, but I was against it. Instead of trying to make it work, they gave up. They should have tried, because they were good influences on each other. Now both of them are worse off than before. My mother won't admit it, but I know she would rather be married to my father now.

CHRIS: Well, I think divorce can be a good thing. My parents were married very young, and over the years my mother outgrew my father intellectually. They're wonderful people but they're very different, and the marriage was destroying them both. They stayed together till I started college, but I think they should have made the break a long time ago.

LYNN: Your parents have only been divorced a few months, so you think of divorce as a way of getting rid of a lot of problems. You'll change your mind when you see that the problems are still there—they're just separated.

CHRIS: I disagree; my mother is much happier now, and I think my father will get used to it and be happier in the long run.

BARBARA: My parents were divorced four years ago and I was completely shocked—they had always seemed like the most loving couple imaginable. One day I was told, "Pack your things. You're going to stay at your aunt's while we get a divorce." My mother married within a few weeks and moved away to Texas.

JON: My father was out of town and sent a letter saying he couldn't live with us anymore. He was really my stepfather, but he'd been with us from the time I was ten until I was sixteen, and I thought of him as my father. It's funny—I say I was shocked, but I must have understood, because for about six months before the letter my behavior foretold the break; I had started cutting school and had become a recluse. Afterward I just gave up on everything for a long time. I had struggled so hard to be a good son to him, so I could have a father and be like everyone else, that I felt betrayed. But it wasn't his fault; my mother was just too strong for him, too intense.

MODERATOR: *What do you feel are the responsibilities of parents to children in a divorce?*

STEVE: I think parents might like to put the children first, but it's not always possible. My father just came home one night very drunk, and he and my mother fought till five in the morning and then he said, "Okay, take your kids and everything else and get out." My mother didn't have a chance to bring us into it. What she did do afterward was marry a man she wasn't in love with so we'd have a roof over our heads. Now she's one of the unhappiest people I know: the only thing that keeps her going is the knowledge that she did it for us. Lately I've been thinking of dropping out of school to study dancing, but I can't do it because it would hurt my mother terribly. She married so that we'd have security, so that I could get a degree, and if I dropped out now, it would be saying that her sacrifice was worthless. I wish she hadn't done it.

BARBARA: My father remarried, but it only lasted six weeks. He did it because he thought my sister and I needed a woman around the house, but we resented her tremendously.

CHRIS: I think you can place too much emphasis on children. My parents spent days explaining the divorce to my twelve-year-old brother, but he couldn't understand a word of it. He thought they were just having a fight and kept asking my father, "But why are you moving out?"

LYNN: I think staying together is very important for the parents if not for the children. People go through a stage in marriage when they want something different. This happens to everyone, but if a couple can try hard to get through this period, the marriage can proceed.

CHRIS: That's ridiculous. The whole purpose of marriage is to bring up a family in a warm, loving atmosphere. If there's no love, no communication, the children will feel the effect—and they might end up by withdrawing from both parents, from everyone.

LYNN: Sure, communication breaks down at certain times
—that's what happened to my parents—but you can live
through that if you work at it.

BARBARA: I think it's very wrong for parents to stay together
or remarry for the sake of the children, but there are ways
of handling a divorce that can make it easier on everyone. For instance, parents should be as honest as they
can be. Even if the children are too young to understand
everything, it's bad if they make a mystery of it. My sister
and I were told we'd get the whole story of the divorce
when we were twenty-one, which is horrible because I
keep thinking it must be for some really terrible reason if
they're going to wait until then.

LYNN: My parents wanted it to be the happiest kind of transition for everyone. They stressed that we were still a
family, and my mother said things like, "Now you'll really
get to know your father because when you see him he'll
be devoting his time to you alone." At that time I thought
yes, you're right, but I hardly see him, and when I do we
aren't any closer.

STEVE: I think parents should be careful not to divorce
themselves from their children. A parent who moves out
should try to keep up real communication; that's what I
yearn for, being able to express my ideas and get a return
from both sides. My father thinks I hate him, but I need
him and always have. He's been out of touch so long he
can't accept that.

BARBARA: Yes, keeping in touch is very important. My
mother is more like a casual friend to me than a mother.
When I talk to her on the phone she says, "I love you, I
miss you," but I can't return that. I don't dislike her, but
how can I love her when I see her twice a year?

ROBIN: My mother lied about my father; she didn't want me
to know what he was like or to love him, and I think that's

an awful thing to do to a child. She gave a party two days after he died, and that hurt me terribly.

MODERATOR: *Have you encountered any special problems because you come from a broken home?*

ROBIN: When I was younger, kids at school made fun of me because I didn't live with my father, but the worst problem was trying to make sense out of the divorce. I listened to my mother's side and then my father's; they were completely different, and it's been hard for me to learn how or why it happened. And I've been lonely almost all of my life. I'm an only child, and my mother has been going through a bad time with the man she's in love with, so I've done a great deal of my own bringing up. My mother loves me, but she hasn't given me much attention—good old tender loving care—and I've been very lonesome. That's why I'm so in love with all my friends; I cherish them with all my might and try to be on my best behavior with them because I feel they're all I've got.

BARBARA: Loneliness is really it for me. I never got accepted by the kids when we moved after the divorce— we've made five moves in three years—and I'm not close to anyone now. When I'm down in the dumps, it's my dogs I go to; they comfort me.

LYNN: With me it's not so much loneliness as being alone. Being self-sufficient. My biggest problem was that my mother leaned on me; I was the person who would understand everything. I didn't want to make her more unhappy with *my* problems, so I had to keep all my own feelings to myself while she used my shoulder to cry on.

JON: That was the hardest thing for me too, being the ear for all my mother's troubles. She has been divorced three times, and each time she poured out everything to me.

Whenever I had a problem it wasn't considered, because she had a more urgent one.

BARBARA: It was different in my house. My older sister got all the problems, but at least she was consulted; I was ignored, and I hated it. My father never confides in me and I feel very left out. But in some ways it may have been harder on my sister. She was sixteen at the time of the divorce and took over the house completely. My father relied on her in all the ways he used to rely on my mother. My sister never really was a teen-ager, and now she's very sophisticated—too sophisticated, I think. The divorce changed our relationship. We used to be close, but when she got so much authority over me I resented it, and we aren't anymore. It wasn't really her fault; my father pushed the responsibility on her because he didn't want to be bothered, and I don't think that was fair.

STEVE: I played housekeeper too. There was no unity at all in our house at the time, and I escaped into the church. I became very religious and identified with Christ the martyr, so I just naturally assumed that role in the house. I didn't have time for any of the things I would have liked to do—to play ball or make real friends; I had to fill my job as martyr.

CHRIS: I really didn't have any problems because my parents' divorce was what I'd call ideal. They were very reasonable and pleasant about it—my mother even continued to do my dad's laundry for a while. Both of them treated me as an adult throughout the whole thing, sort of as a mediator, in fact. And now when I see them there's no conflict; I love them both and I try to help them both.

ROBIN: You're lucky. I had a hard time making my parents understand that I love them both equally, if for different reasons. My father would ask, "What can you see in your mother? She's so mean." And my mother would tell me he was irresponsible and immature and I should forget him. I was really torn; I didn't know what to think.

LYNN: That's very bad. I was always told, "No matter what your father did to me, he's still your father and you should love him."

BARBARA: Well, I have a lot of resentment against my father even though I live with him, because after the divorce he just stopped trying to be a father to me. Before the divorce I had anything I wanted within reason, but now if I want a new dress or something, it's, "Well, we'll think about it." Money has become a problem and that doesn't help my resentment.

JON: One of the things I've always envied about people who don't come from broken homes is their security and naturalness. That comes from living with parents who enjoy being around each other and have built up something so strong you feel you could push off from it, that nothing you do can ever knock it down. I can't say, "I hate you," to my mother in an argument, for instance, because I know it may really upset her.

ROBIN: I know what you mean, but I don't regret having only one parent, because there are advantages. For one thing, my mother can't say, "Wait till your father comes home and I tell him about you," or, "You'll have to ask your father if you can do that." From what I've seen in some of my friends' homes, it's harder for them; they have to listen to both sides all the time, whether they like it or not.

STEVE: Well, I envy my friends who have two parents because they know about love and a family and they can really question their parents. I can't; I have to be very careful not to touch on the inadequacies they feel because of the divorce.

LYNN: I've found myself tending to build my own security. I've had to depend on myself more and more and I really have my own ideas on things. After the divorce my younger brother became more dependent on me, and the two of us are building a family around ourselves.

MODERATOR: *How do you feel about your parents' dating and remarrying?*

ROBIN: I used to hate it when my mother had dates; she paid more attention to them than to me. But now that I'm older, I'd like her to remarry—it would take the heat off me, and it would be nice to have a man around the house.

CHRIS: One of the biggest thrills of my life was the night my mother spent two and a half hours on the phone with a man. She still hasn't heard the end of it! I think she may have some of the same problems if she remarries; sometimes I think she's searching for an ideal man who doesn't exist—but I hope she'll be able to find someone she can be happy with.

LYNN: My father has already remarried—a woman who's as unlike my mother as someone can be. Instead of solving his problems he seems to have accentuated them because he chose someone who was different rather than right for him.

BARBARA: My father dates a lot and I make jokes about getting his girls and the messages straight—"Tell Kay I'm sleeping; if Nancy calls I'm out," and so on—but I really hate it. And when I think of my friends who don't have to lie for their fathers and who have real happiness at home, I can't stand it. I'd like him to remarry because he's going to need someone, but not till I'm out of the house. My mother's husband tries so hard to be nice to me that it annoys me, because I know it's an act. I don't want to have to deal with a stepmother too.

JON: Well, I welcomed the men my mother dated and married. The man she's serious about now is a great guy, and I'm trying to get them set together and make her understand that she's got to be a woman and not try to be everything.

STEVE: In the beginning my stepfather played a good role. He offered security and he was a father to me, and I respected him for that. He had been in the army and he ran his home that way. We had curfews, KP duty, floor detail, the works. I really loved it; we all did. But when he began to feel my mother was using him, he started drinking and got very belligerent. Then I resented his telling us what to do, though when I was younger I liked it.

MODERATOR: *Can any of you see yourselves divorced in the future?*

BARBARA: Definitely. I can picture it a lot sooner than I can see myself happily married. Divorce is really the only pattern I know.

JON: I can see myself divorced, but it has nothing to do with my background. It's just that I don't believe you can ever know beforehand if you're really suited for marriage to a particular person. I can see divorce as the logical, mature thing to do if we found that we weren't really in love—if we just enjoyed each other's company but weren't involved anymore.

LYNN: I can never imagine myself divorced, never!

ROBIN: I don't think I will be either because I've learned not to go along with the idea so many people have—my mother had it—that to be married means to raise a family. People who marry to have a family and find that they can't get along with their partner end up by inflicting things on their kids. I'm going to marry whether I can have a family or not, because I love the man and want to live with him, even if he wouldn't be a good father. I know lots of married couples with beautiful relationships who never think of having children.

JON: Everyone thinks that love matters most, children or not. But there has to be economic stability and emotional equilibrium as well—each person secure in himself. Love is about fifty per cent of what it takes; the other things are the rest, and neither half will suffice without the other.

CHRIS: That's right, because love, even true love, doesn't last forever. There comes a point after, say, ten years of living together when it just can't be that exciting anymore. And then problems, lack of money for instance, that might have been insignificant in the beginning will become tremendously important.

LYNN: We never had enough money—who does?—but that can be an asset to a family. It was a common problem and in the early years we all worked together on it. Money isn't such a big deal. Why worry about it or turn your life inside out for it? A marriage needs love and a structured feeling, the idea that the family unit is worth working for, worth keeping.

MODERATOR: *How has your parents' divorce changed you?*

ROBIN: From what I've seen, the most obvious thing that happens to children from broken homes is that they grow up faster. Everyone who meets me is amazed to find that I'm only fourteen; I'm much older emotionally because of the divorce, because I've been independent for a long time, except economically. If you don't have two parents holding your hands, one hand is free, and you use it to reach out, to do things with, to think for yourself.

CHRIS: My parents' divorce has made me aware of the intricacies of marriage—that it's not some sort of fairy tale in which everyone lives happily ever after. I think this is good and that a boy or girl who comes out of a divorce without being seriously hurt by it has a chance to see his parents are real people, which can be a beautiful thing. I've gained tremendous insight about my mother just by meeting the men she dates. And I've learned that marriage is an artificial thing; it's nice if it works, but if it doesn't there's no point in sticking together.

STEVE: I think my experience will make me more tolerant of my wife's faults, rather than quicker to ask for a divorce. I'm going to try harder to stick it out, not so much for any children we might have but because I'd like to overcome my parents' faults.

BARBARA: I'm afraid of marriage. I find that when I really start to like a boy, I make some excuse to break it up. I have a friend whose parents are divorced who's just the opposite; she wants the security she misses at home.

JON: My mother was like that. I'm a second-generation child of divorce. She and my father got married for security, and when they didn't find it in each other they pinned their hopes on me. Their divorce has made me certain that I won't marry till I'm about forty, till I'm sure I'm not marrying just to find security in a wife or in children. Children are supposed to come because you want them for themselves, not because you can't hold a job or are a failure socially and suddenly decide you can find fulfillment in being a parent.

LYNN: You all make it sound as if you learned about marriage because your parents are divorced. I don't think teen-agers from normal homes have such an unrealistic idea of marriage in the first place, and I know I'd have learned more about marriage if my parents hadn't divorced, if I could have seen them working out their problems. But I am different now. For one thing, I don't want to go out with anyone who's the least bit like my father. At the same time, oddly enough, I've really pinpointed the things I admire in him, things I wasn't aware of before the divorce.

STEVE: I've become more selective and cautious about dating too. My parents were both very good-looking, but I know better than to marry for superficial reasons. My mother left college to marry my father, and when he didn't become a success in business she blamed him for bringing her down in the world. I'm going to marry a career girl so she can never accuse me of making her give up anything.

LYNN: Well, if I've learned one thing about choosing a husband, it's that communication—not looks, not money or even common interests—is the most important thing.

BARBARA: If I do marry I'm going to want security, economic security and the feeling my husband is someone I can really trust. Since the divorce I've become suspicious and analytical about my friends—I can see right through a girl who's going to be false to me. It's as if because I need someone to depend on and confide in so badly I look deeper into people; I can't stand anyone who'll say one thing and do another.

JON: Yes, I've come to despise any kind of artificiality or weakness that people bring on themselves, like drinking too much. This is really hypocritical of me because all of us are weak in some way, but it angers me to the point that I don't want to get involved with anyone who's going to mess himself up and involve me in it. I don't let anyone get really close to me anymore. I suppose being rejected by my stepfather has made me that way.

CHRIS: I know what you mean, but I think I'd be worse off if my parents had stayed together. Those last few years my mother was really becoming neurotic, and it's a terrible thing to see someone you love become warped and bitter.

BARBARA: We always seemed like a close family, and I think if my parents hadn't divorced I'd have been a warmer, more loving person than I am. I'm wary or maybe cynical about people, especially boys. Part of it is that I don't have a clear feeling of who I am or what I want.

JON: It's odd—almost all of us are lonely, cautious, a little bit hard toward people, as if we're afraid to have close relationships for fear they'll turn out like our parents' marriages. Yet Steve wants to be a dancer, Barbara wants to act and I want to be a musician. We want to entertain people, to relate to them. You'd think we'd all be more interested in ivory tower careers but we're not; I guess we've adjusted.

MODERATOR: *What can you do to adjust well to divorce in the family?*

BARBARA: You have to be honest with yourself. That's the main thing. Accept divorce, that it's happened and that you can't put the marriage back together again. And if you can't learn to live with one of your parents and like it, you should start thinking of yourself and the life you want in an adult fashion. This is a lot of responsibility, but if you really want to come out whole, you can do it. If you don't try, it's just as much your fault as your parents'.

LYNN: It's even more than that. A lot of kids use divorce as an excuse, a crutch. They say, "My parents are divorced so I've really got it tough—don't expect much of me." But not only do you have to help yourself; you have to help everyone around you because it's your family, divorce or not.

JON: You should think of it as something in your parents'

life, not your own, and realize that it isn't your fault and you can't do anything to bring them together. I felt terribly inadequate because I couldn't do that. I was very young and I didn't have the power to look at the situation objectively. But as I got older I developed it; anyone can. It's just like learning something in school. I finally came to see that that's the way life often is.

STEVE: Age isn't the biggest factor in adjusting to divorce; it's attitude. And what you start with as a person. My older brother, for instance, blamed my parents for everything that ever went wrong after the divorce. He dropped out of high school, and now he feels the world owes him something. I was lucky because I was sort of the number one child. I had a lot of approval, so when the storm broke I didn't get knocked down. Because I had already proved myself in a sense, my parents' problems weren't the end of my world.

LYNN: You have to use a bad situation to your advantage. In my case, for instance, I can really benefit from seeing my mother and father as separate people. It's as if I get a fuller picture from being in two different environments, and I'm more tolerant of other people with differences or faults—I can still see the good in them.

ROBIN: We're the only ones who can decide how we'll be affected by a divorce—nothing parents say or do can help if you've made up your mind to use it as an excuse for getting away with things or making yourself miserable.

JON: Yes. I was negative for a long time, but I finally decided there was no point in it. It's a very draggy, painful way to be. Self-pity can be an absorbing game for a while, but it's really a waste of time.

NOTES, REFERENCES, BIBLIOGRAPHIES

PROLOGUE

Arnstein, Helene S. *What To Tell Your Child,* Indianapolis and New York: The Bobbs-Merrill Company, Inc., 1960.

Blaine, Graham B., Jr. "Children of Divorce," in *Atlantic Monthly,* March 1963.

——. *Youth and the Hazards of Affluence.* New York and London: Harper and Row, 1966, pp. 14–19 and 22.

Burgess, E. W., and Cottrell, L. S. *Predicting Success or Failure in Marriage,* New York: Prentice-Hall, 1939.

Burgess, Ernest, and Locke, Harvey J. *The Family,* New York: American Book Company, 1945.

Camper, Shirley. *How To Get Along With Your Child,* New York: Belmont Books, 1962.

Champagne, Marion. *Facing Life Alone,* Indianapolis and New York: The Bobbs-Merrill Company, Inc., 1964.

Cunningham, Glenn. "Motivating Children Toward Desirable Goals," in *The Single Parent,* December 1966.

Despert, J. Louise. *Children of Divorce,* Garden City, New York: Doubleday and Company, 1953.

Emerson, James G., Jr. *Divorce, The Church, and Remarriage,* Philadelphia: The Westminster Press, 1961.

Freid, Jacob. *Jews and Divorce,* New York: Ktav Publishing House, Inc., 1968.

Ginott, Haim G. *Between Parent and Child,* New York: The Macmillan Company, 1967.

Goode, William J. *After Divorce,* New York: Free Press, 1956.

——. "Family Disorganization," in *Contemporary Social Problems,* edited by Robert K. Merton and Robert A. Nisbet. New York: Harcourt, Brace and World, Inc., 1961.

——. "Family Disorganization," in *Contemporary Social Problems,* second edition, edited by Robert K. Merton and Robert A. Nisbet. New York: Harcourt, Brace and World, Inc., 1966.

——. *Women in Divorce,* New York: Free Press, 1965.

Gordis, Robert. *Sex and the Family in the Jewish Tradition,* New York: The Burning Bush Press, 1967.

Greene, Bernard L. *The Psychotherapies of Marital Disharmony,* New York: The Free Press, 1965.

Haussamen, Florence, and Guitar, Mary Anne. *The Divorce Handbook,* New York: G. P. Putnam's Sons, 1960.

Hulme, William E. *The Pastoral Care of Families,* New York and Nashville: Abingdon Press, 1962.

Hunt, Morton M. "Wanted: Divorce Counselors," in *The Single Parent,* February-March 1967.

——. *The World of the Formerly Married,* New York: McGraw-Hill Book Company, 1966.

Ilg, Francis L., and Ames, Louise Bates. *The Gesell Institute's: Parents Ask,* New York: Dell Publishing Company, 1962.

Jacobson, Paul H. *American Marriage and Divorce,* New York: Rinehart, 1959.

Johnson, Paul E. *Psychology of Pastoral Care,* New York and Nashville: Abingdon Press, 1953.

Joseph, Harry, and Zern, Gordon. *The Emotional Problems of Children,* New York: Crown Publishers, Inc., 1954.

Kaye, Robert E. "Children Are Human Beings," in *The Single Parent,* July 1966.

Langer, Marion. *Learning To Live as a Widow,* New York: Gilbert Press, Inc., 1957.

Lepp, Ignace. *The Psychology of Loving,* New York: Helicon Press, Inc., 1963.

Mayer, Michael F. *Divorce and Annulment,* New York: Arco Publishing Company, Inc., 1967.

Metz, Charles V. *Divorce and Custody for Men,* Garden City, New York: Doubleday and Company, Inc., 1968.

Missildine, W. Hugh. *Your Inner Child of the Past,* New York: Simon and Schuster, 1963.

Morrissey, Jim. "Compassion and Understanding," in *The Single Parent,* April 1967.

Mudd, Emily H. *Marriage Counseling: A Casebook,* New York: Association Press, 1958.

Ogg, Elizabeth. *Divorce,* Public Affairs Pamphlet No. 380, 1965.

Reynolds, William F. "A Counselor's Notebook," in *The Single Parent,* April 1966.

Spock, Benjamin. *Problems of Parents,* Boston: Houghton Mifflin Company, 1962.

Terman, L. M. *Psychological Factors in Marital Happiness,* New York: McGraw-Hill, 1938.

"A Time Essay" in *Time, The Weekly News-Magazine,* February 11, 1966.

Wolf, Anna M. W. and Stein, Lucille. *The One-Parent Family,* Public Affairs Pamphlet No. 287, 1959.

CHAPTER I

1. For good illustrative materials see, among else, J. Louise Despert, *Children of Divorce,* Garden City, New York: Doubleday, 1953; and James S. Plant, "The Psychiatrist Views Children of Divorced Parents," *Law and Contemporary Problems,* X, 1944, pp. 807–818.

2. See, for example, Edward Pokorny, "Observations by a 'Friend of the Court,'" *Law and Contemporary Problems,* X, 1944, pp. 778–789.

3. Kingsley Davis, "Children of Divorced Parents: Sociological and Statistical Analysis," *Law and Contemporary Problems,* X, 1944, pp. 700–720.

4. See for instance: Norman B. Bernstein and John S. Robey, "The Detection and Management of Pediatric Difficulties Created by Divorce," *Pediatrics,* Dec. 1962, pp. 950–956.

5. Statistical information mentioned in the discussion is, unless otherwise specified, based on the 1960 U.S. Census of Population.

6. Paul H. Jacobson, *American Marriage and Divorce,* New York: Rinehart & Co., 1959, p. 135.

7. For a further discussion see: Jetse Sprey, "The Study of Single-Parenthood: Some Methodological Considerations," *The Family Life Coordinator,* XVI, 1967, pp. 29–34.

8. Judson T. Landis, "The Trauma of Children When Parents Divorce," *Marriage and Family Living,* XXII, 1960, p. 7.

9. Morris Rosenberg, *Society and the Adolescent Self-Image,* Princeton, New Jersey: Princeton Univ. Press, 1965.

10. *Ibid.,* pp. 96–98.

11. Sheldon and Eleanor Glueck, *Unraveling Juvenile Delinquency,* Cambridge, Mass.: Harvard University Press, 1960.

12. See: Charles E. Bowerman and Donald P. Irish, "Some Relationships of Stepchildren to Their Parents," *Marriage and Family Living,* XXIV, 1962, pp. 113–128; also, Margaret B. Koch, "Anxiety in Preschool Children," *Merrill-Palmer Quarterly,* VII, 1961, pp. 225–231.

13. T. S. Langner and S. T. Michael, *Life Stress and Mental Health,* New York: The Free Press of Glencoe, 1963.

14. Goode, William J. *Women in Divorce,* New York: The Free Press, 1965, chapter XXI.

15. Ivan F. Nye, "Child Adjustment in Broken and in Unhappy Unbroken Homes," *Marriage and Family Living,* XIX, 1957, pp. 356–361.

16. Judson T. Landis, *op. cit.*

17. Lee Burchinal, "Characteristics of Adolescents from Unbroken, Broken, and Reconstituted Families," *Journal of Marriage and the Family,* XXVI, 1964, pp. 44–51.

18. Jacobson, *op. cit.,* p. 87.

19. Goode, *op. cit.,* pp. 280–281.

20. Morton M. Hunt, *The World of the Formerly Married,* New York: McGraw-Hill, 1966, pp. 260–261 and 278–279; and Despert, *op. cit.,* Section II.

21. Rosenberg, *op. cit.,* pp. 98–104.

22. Langner and Michael, *op. cit.*

23. Bowerman and Irish, *op. cit.,* p. 121.

24. Jessie Bernard, *Remarriage,* New York: Dryden Press, 1956, pp. 318–329.

25. Goode, *op. cit.,* p. 329.

CHAPTER II

1. Earl A. Grollman, ed. *Explaining Death to Children,* Boston: Beacon Press, 1967.

2. Louis Nizer, *My Life in Court,* New York: Doubleday, 1941.

3. K. Chukovsky, *From Two to Five,* Berkeley: U. of California Press, 1963; and E. Pitcher, and E. Prelinger, *Children Tell Stories: An Analysis of Fantasy,* New York: International Universities Press, 1963.

4. Erik Erikson, *Childhood and Society,* New York: Norton Press, 1951.

5. Evelyn W. Goodenough, "Interest in Persons as an Aspect of Sex Difference in the Early Years," *Genetic Psych. Monogr.,* LV, 1957, pp. 287–323.

6. George Frank, "The Role of the Family in the Development of Psychopathology," *Psych. Bulletin* LXIV, no. 3, 1965, pp. 191–205.

7. J. M. Tanner and B. Inhelder, *Discussions on Child Development,* vol. II, New York: International Universities Press, 1954.

CHAPTER IV

1. It is possible to see how Jeff might have drawn the conclusion that his resentment of Ron magically caused his disappearance. This was, of course, his first "real" confrontation with the triangular Oedipal drama. Guilt over Oedipal strivings leads some children, even when secure in familial love and treated kindly, to fantasy the most fiendish retaliations directed against themselves for relatively minor offenses. Nightmares,

the "universal neurosis of children," are examples of such psychological mechanisms. Poets and novelists have noted the relationship of horrifying dreams to the state of going to bed in anger.

2. How one helps children to understand the concept of adoption is an individual matter. The general practice of telling a child "the truth" that he is adopted as soon as he asks, should be thought over carefully and adapted to the particular case. Increasing curiosity and attendant fantasies about his own origin may be extremely supportive or destructive in terms of enhancing or detracting from a child's sense of self-value. In the very young the story of adoption (often insistently thrust upon a child out of parental need to assuage guilt), the fact that he came from some place else and had a different father or mother, can only increase anxiety and confusion. An important reason for this is the inability of the small child to understand the facts of pregnancy and birth. To him, such phenomena can hardly be differentiated from the processes of intake and elimination of food. It might be of interest to know that many times a child who has been told he was adopted often thinks either that he damaged his real parents by his birth, or he was defective and thus given up by his real parents (Oedipus, the club-footed one!), or that his parents were murdered or kidnapped, or that he himself was kidnapped by his adoptive parents. According to Peller, all children who have been enlightened about their adoption under 8 years of age, have had gross misconceptions about the events and the persons involved in their birth and subsequent adoption. She suggests that "birth-parent" and "birth-mother" are better terms than either "real mother" or "natural mother." In her opinion "the adoptive parents, who love and provide for the child, are doing something natural and biological." Jeff's mother seems to have made use of this concept in her own way when she told him he had a "real daddy" in Murray.

The best period for telling a child he is adopted is probably during the latency period, early in his school years. This is a time when many of the terrifying pre-Oedipal and Oedipal fantasies have given way to more romantic and cherished fantasies that their real parents are not their own. Such fantasies, coming probably about as compensations for feelings of alienation, for small rejections or frustrations, and conflicts over the issues of daily life, assure the child that he had been the son of royalty or of another, richer family, things would have been otherwise! His "own" parents had been a better set altogether! Paradoxically, the adopted child in the latency period, finds it easier, even consoling, therefore to accept the story of his adoption since he can safely fantasy "my real mother, or father, would have done differently; *they* would not have treated me so." It seems true that during these latency years fantasies of this sort are not ultimately destructive of self value. To wait until the child is adolescent to inform him he is adopted is most unwise.

CHAPTER VI

1. *New England Journal of Medicine,* June 8, 1967.
2. Louise J. Despert, *Children of Divorce,* Garden City, New York: Doubleday, 1953.

CHAPTER VII

1. William L. O'Neill, *Divorce in a Progressive Era,* New Haven: Yale Press, 1967, p. 30.
2. J. L. Schulman, *Management of Emotional Disorders in Pediatric Practice,* Chicago: Yearbook Medical Publishers, 1967, pp. 142 ff.
3. Judson Landis, "The Trauma of Children Where Parents Divorce," *Marriage and Family Living,* 1960, 22, pp. 7–13.
4. Graham B. Blaine, Jr., *Youth and The Hazards of Affluence,* New York: Harper and Row, 1967, p. 15.
5. Blaine, *op. cit.,* p. 18.
6. Gregory Rochlin, *Griefs and Discontents,* Boston: Little, Brown and Company, 1965, p. 45.
7. William J. Goode, *After Divorce,* Glencoe, Illinois: Free Press, 1956, p. 318.

8. Blaine, *op. cit.,* p. 20.

9. Jessie Bernard, *Remarriage,* New York: Dryden Press, 1956, p. 11.

10. Goode, *op. cit.,* p. 308

CHAPTER VIII

1. U.S. Bureau of the Census, *Statistical Abstract of the United States: 1967,* 88th ed., Washington, D.C., 1967.

2. Thomas Langner and Stanley T. Michael, *Life Stress and Mental Health: The Midtown Manhattan Study,* vol. II, New York: Free Press of Glencoe, 1963.

3. John L. Thomas, *Religion and the American People,* Westminster, Maryland: The Newman Press, 1963.

4. John L. Thomas, *Catholic Viewpoint on Marriage and the Family,* rev. ed., Garden City, New York: Doubleday & Company, 1965.

5. John L. Thomas, *The American Catholic Family,* Englewood Cliffs, New Jersey: Prentice-Hall, 1956.

6. C. G. Vernier, *American Family Law,* 5 vols., Stanford University, California: Stanford University Press, 1938; T. Lincoln Bouscaren, and Adam C. Ellis, *Canon Law: A Text and Commentary,* rev. ed., Milwaukee: Bruce Publishing Company, 1951.

7. Divorce: A Re-examination of Basic Concepts. *Law and Contemporary Problems,* vol. 18, Durham, North Carolina: School of Law, Duke University, 1953.

8. William J. Goode, *After Divorce,* Glencoe, Illinois: The Free Press, 1956.

9. Louise J. Despert, *Children of Divorce,* Garden City, New Jersey: Doubleday & Company, 1963.

10. William J. Goode, *The Family,* Englewood Cliffs, New Jersey: Prentice-Hall, 1964.

11. Anne W. Simon, *Stepchild in the Family,* New York: The Odyssey Press, 1964.

12. Jessie Bernard, *Remarriage,* New York: The Dryden Press, 1956.

13. Marjorie P. Ilgenfritz, "Mothers on Their Own—Widows and Divorcees," *Journal of Marriage and the Family,* XXIII, 1961, pp. 38–41.

14. Jim Egelson and Janet F. Egelson, *Parents Without Partners: One-Parent Families,* Public Affairs Pamphlet No. 287, New York: 1959.

15. Patricia Coleman, "Divorced Catholics," *U.S. Catholic,* September 1965, pp. 6–11.

16. Victor J. Pospishil, *Divorce and Remarriage,* New York: Herder and Herder, 1967.

CHAPTER IX

Allport, Gordon W. *The Individual and His Religion,* New York: The Macmillan Company, 1960.

Barish, Louis and Rebecca. *Basic Jewish Beliefs,* New York: Jonathan-David, 1961.

Bokser, Ben Zion. *The Wisdom of the Talmud,* New York: Philosophical Library, 1951.

Brav, Stanley R., and Falk, Randall M. *The Family: The Jewish View,* Department of Adult Jewish Education, Union of American Hebrew Congregations, November 16, 1963.

Cohen, A. *Everyman's Talmud,* New York: E. P. Dutton & Co., Inc., 1949.

Cohen, Simon. "Divorce," *The Universal Jewish Encyclopedia,* vol. III. New York: Universal Jewish Encyclopedia Company, Inc., 1941.

Cohon, Samuel S. *Judaism, A Way of Life,* Cincinnati: Union of American Hebrew Congregations, 1948.

"Divorce," *The Jewish Encyclopedia,* vol. IV. New York and London: Funk and Wagnalls Company, 1902.

Divorce, Resolution adopted by the General Assembly of the Union of American Hebrew Congregations, November 14–17, 1965.

Emerson, James G., Jr. *Divorce, the Church, and Remarriage,* Philadelphia: The Westminster Press, 1961.

Freehof, Solomon B. *Reform Jewish Practice,* Cincinnati: Hebrew Union College Press, 1944.

Freid, Jacob, editor. *Jews and Divorce,* New York: Ktav Publishing House, Inc., 1968.

Fromm, Erich. *The Art of Loving,* New York: Bantam Books, Inc., 1963.

Gittelsohn, Roland B. *Consecrated Unto Me,* New York: Union of American Hebrew Congregations, 1965.

Goldstein, Albert S. "Should We Give a Get?" in *Central Conference of American Rabbis Journal,* June 1967.

———. *What Is Man?* Message of Union of American Hebrew Congregations, September 13, 1964.

Gordis, Robert. *Sex and the Family in the Jewish Tradition,* New York: The Burning Bush Press, 1967.

———. "The Jewish View on Birth Control, Divorce, and Marriage," in *Jewish Heritage,* Fall 1967.

Green, Alan Singer. *The Delight Between Husband and Wife: A Jewish Ideal,* Message of Israel, May 13, 1962. Radio series.

Grollman, Earl A. *Rabbinical Counseling,* New York: Bloch Publishing Company, 1966.

Horowitz, George. *The Spirit of Jewish Law,* New York: Central Book Company, 1953.

Hulme, William E. *The Pastoral Care of Families,* New York and Nashville: Abingdon Press, 1962.

Johnson, Paul E. *Psychology of Pastoral Care,* New York and Nashville: Abingdon Press, 1953.

Landau, Sol. "The Jewish Interpretation of Love," in *The National Jewish Monthly,* LXXVI, no. 4, December 1961.

Levy, Felix A. *Judaism and Marriage,* Popular Studies in Judaism Pamphlet 19. Union of American Hebrew Congregations.

Linn, Louis, and Schwarz, Leo W. *Psychiatry and Religious Experience,* New York: Random House, 1958.

"The Magnetic Attraction of Mixed Dating," in *Central Conference of American Rabbis Journal,* April 1964.

Mescheloff, Moses. *The Parting of Ways,* Chicago: Rabbinical Council.

———. *Procedure in Obtaining a Religious Jewish Divorce,* Chicago Rabbinical Council.

Mihaly, Eugene. "The Jewish View of Marriage," in *Central Conference of American Rabbis Journal,* October 1954.

Moore, George Foot. *Judaism,* vol. I, II. Cambridge: Harvard University Press, 1946.

Ostow, Mortimer, and Scharfstein, Ben Ami. *The Need to Believe,* New York: International Universities Press, Inc., 1954.

Patai, Raphael. *Family, Love and The Bible,* London: Macgibbon and Kee, 1960.

Petuchowski, Jacob J. "Some Reflections on the Reform Jewish Attitude Towards Divorce," in *Central Conference of American Rabbis Journal.*

Pool, David de Sola. *Why I Am a Jew,* New York: Bloch Publishing Company, 1957.

Rabinowitz, Stanley R. *A Jewish View of Love and Marriage,* Judaism Pamphlet Series; B'nai B'rith Youth Organization.

Raddock, Charles. "MOs and FMs Are Dancing Toward Altar (they hope)," in *The National Jewish Monthly,* March 1968.

Rosenberg, Stuart. *More Loves Than One,* New York: Thomas Nelson and Sons, 1963.

Shapiro, Manheim. *Jewish family values: are they breaking down—or shifting? American Jewish Committee,* November 1965.

Shoulson, Abraham B. *Marriage and Family Life: A Jewish View,* New York: Twayne Publishers, 1959.

Shulman, Albert M. *Report of the Central Conference of American Rabbis Committee on Marriage, Family, and Home,* Philadelphia, 1964.

Simon, Rhoda B., and Trainin, Isaac N. "Can We Stem the Rise of Divorce in American Jewry?" in *The Jewish Digest,* June 1967.

Smith, Harold P. *K'dushin—Holy Matrimony,* Chicago Rabbinical Council.

Stewart, Charles William. "Counseling the Divorcee," in *Pastoral Psychology,* XIV, no. 133, April 1963.

Stoffer, Ruth Mallay. "Love, Marriage, Divorce Face Crisis in Our Time," in *The National Jewish Monthly,* October 1967.

"The Widow, the Divorcee, and the Single Woman," in *Pastoral Psychology,* XVIII, no. 179, December 1967.